WHY HER? WHY NOT ME?

A Series of Deep Familial Misfortunes,
Including the Loss of Two Wives, Tests
The Mettle of an Advanced-Aged
Father Charged with Raising Two Sets
of Generationally-Separated Children

Roland J. Bain

BALBOA.
PRESS

A DIVISION OF HAY HOUSE

Balboa Press books may be ordered through booksellers or by contacting:

Balboa Press
A Division of Hay House
1663 Liberty Drive
Bloomington, IN 47403
www.balboapress.com
1 (877) 407-4847

Because of the dynamic nature of the Internet, any web addresses or links contained in this book may have changed since publication and may no longer be valid. The views expressed in this work are solely those of the author and do not necessarily reflect the views of the publisher, and the publisher hereby disclaims any responsibility for them.

The author of this book does not dispense medical advice or prescribe the use of any technique as a form of treatment for physical, emotional, or medical problems without the advice of a physician, either directly or indirectly. The intent of the author is only to offer information of a general nature to help you in your quest for emotional and spiritual well-being. In the event you use any of the information in this book for yourself, which is your constitutional right, the author and the publisher assume no responsibility for your actions.

Any people depicted in stock imagery provided by Getty Images are models, and such images are being used for illustrative purposes only.
Certain stock imagery © Getty Images.

Print information available on the last page.

ISBN: 978-1-9822-0944-5 (sc)
ISBN: 978-1-9822-0943-8 (hc)
ISBN: 978-1-9822-0945-2 (e)

Library of Congress Control Number: 2018909078

Balboa Press rev. date: 08/30/2018

Contents

CHAPTER 1

THE FIRST TRAUMATIC EVENT

During those infrequent occasions when I call a time-out to reflect on life, I marvel at the human being's ability to survive life's pitfalls and traumatic events. In my case, I've survived two wives leaving me and our children. In the first case I had the mission of singly raising 5 children and in the second, only two. After 17 years of marriage my first wife divorced me and gave me full custody of our children. I was 44-years-old. My second wife, the mother of our two children was 27 years my junior. At the time of our marriage she was 25-years-old; I was 52. At the time of her traumatic departure I was 74-years-old. I can readily add to life's pitfalls and traumatic events, the ugly role that cancer played in our lives and the blessing of survival, at least for some of us.

The events surrounding my second marriage serve as the central premise of these writings.

My first wife and I met while we were students at UCLA. She was a business major, and I, a petroleum geology major. She was a member of a sorority and I, a fraternity, the link having facilitated our meeting each other. Once we realized we were in love, the traditional sequence of events commenced, beginning with our becoming "pinned." A year later we were married, this followed by the arrival of our first child the following year (1956). Just prior to our son's birth I was notified that I had been awarded a Fulbright Scholarship to conduct research for a year at the French Petroleum Institute near Paris, France.

We were faced with a dilemma; to accept or to decline? It was a difficult decision to make. After much discussion, we decided to accept the award and to prepare ourselves for this new adventure. Our son was two months old when we arrived in Paris. After adjusting to the new lifestyle and culture, we enjoyed this great adventure.

During the next five years the other children, including twins, were born at roughly two-year intervals, with the result that we had 5 children under 5-years-old. It's safe to say that we didn't have much free time.

As the years passed and the children grew older, my wife decided to return to college. My having my office in our home facilitated her taking late afternoon and early evening classes. Even before she received a Master's Degree in psychology, she joined a group in her department whose mission was to formulate a program specifically designed for the police department. A special group of police officers were to be trained to counsel problem students at various school campuses.

Her absence from home grew in tempo with her involvement in the program. As time and events progressed, it became clear that our marriage was in distress. The minimal amount of counseling we tried did not help. After 17 years of marriage she made the decision to seek a divorce.

The day my wife moved out I felt as if a huge hole had opened and swallowed me whole. It seemed as if my brain activity ceased and numbness filled my body. Life no longer held importance for me. And I couldn't have been more ill-prepared to face the future that awaited the children and me, a future that frightened me.

Having to be available 24/7 for the children was highly demanding. How does a person learn to manage a household overnight? How do you learn to prepare meals with virtually no notice, let alone having no experience? With the two-story house came many responsibilities. Doling out the chores brought with it yelps of unfairness, allusions to child-labor laws, and the like. To a degree. the system I devised for the children worked, which helped to ease my workload. Also, the fact that they were good-to-excellent students, was another factor that eased some of the burden. Having one daughter and four boys, of course, presented other problems. She was involved in much of the bickering and complaining, some of this in self-defense. All too often she was an easy target for her brothers. Without question, we needed an adult woman in the house.

From the outset, the tasks of preparing meals and doing the related shopping were challenges for me. I began trying to scope out a week's worth of meals at a time. My twelve-year-old daughter chipped in as best she could. Her specialty was tuna casserole and I let her make it whenever she felt like it. I'm surprised that we still like tuna, casserole!

My mother also had been a blessing. Periodically, she would spend several days with us during which time she would cook up a storm until we had a freezer full of dinners. Also, because she was a world-class seamstress, the mending pile would disappear during her visits.

My office was in my home at that time, which made for a convenient arrangement, at least to a point. While the children were in school it was easy enough to get some work done. When the children were at home, though, distractions were many and often. It was not an environment conducive to working.

Following a lengthy period of intermittent contact with her children, my ex-wife began interacting more closely with her children by having them occasionally join her for dinner at her apartment. In time, this led to them having dinner with her on Sundays. Regardless of my personal feelings, I began looking forward to Sundays. Any and all relief in the meal-preparation department was gratefully accepted.

At the time of my wife's departure, the age of the children ranged from 10 to 15 years. The timing of her departure coincided with the early phase of the 1960s/1970s drug culture (the Haight-Ashbury, Flower Child, Free Love culture), as well as the ushering in of the anti-Establishment era. Another element of the new and growing culture was the "if it feels good, do it" mantra. What a challenge all of this was for me, a product of old-school thinking.

Even in this chaos-filled lifestyle, at the end of the day I was beginning to experience increasing loneliness. The children had their friends and outside activities to keep them busy. Often enough I was tempted to visit a local bistro just to mingle with adults. And with my office located in my house, the potential for interacting with adults, other than on the phone, was minimal.

Yes, the divorce and custody of five children had plunged me into a huge emotional hole. My ego was crushed. There I was at age forty-four with virtually no social life. Eventually, however, I did start dating, thanks in large part to friends setting me up with blind dates. As reluctant I was to engage in blind dates, I did enjoy the female companionship. I learned early that it was highly unlikely that a serious relationship could develop with those I dated, primarily because each of them had been married, and each had custody of a child or children. I certainly wasn't looking to add children to my already-substantial brood. Of course, I doubt that anyone I dated was interested in marrying into a family of five children, essentially each of them a teenager.

Until I started dating I hadn't realized that divorce was so prevalent. I felt sorry for most of those I dated as they seemed to be experiencing the same trauma that I had endured. As in my case, they were struggling for survival. Because of my own experiences at home, I also pitied their children.

Five years after my wife had divorced me and had giving me full custody of our children, I was a very tired and depressed soul. The never-ending demands of maintaining our home and the needs of my children, had an impact on my consultancy. Too often my heart just was not into meeting the obligations of my work. This had to change.

Even though it was a tumultuous and hugely demanding time for me, one of the greatest events in my life was about to happen —meeting the one of the finest and loveliest persons I've had the pleasure to meet. There was no way that I could have divined the incredible events that would follow.

CHAPTER 2

MEETING NANCY AND DOES AGE DIFFERENCE REALLY MATTER?

One of the greatest blessings of my life happened five years after my wife of 17years left me and our 5 children -- I met Nancy. What a God send! I met her on her first day of employment in a men's clothing store. I won't say it was love at first sight, but I was really impressed the moment I saw her. Without question, this very attractive young woman activated my emotional center.

What an engaging smile I received as she approached and asked if she could be of assistance. Thanks to her, the shopping experience was one to remember. She was so refreshing and outgoing. All too soon it was time to pay. As we headed to the cash register I asked her name. A cheerful, "Nancy", was her answer. I responded with, "My name's Roland, and please try to remember it." My smile was in concert with hers. I then asked how long she had worked at the store. I was surprised when she said it was her first day. "Oh my gosh", I said, "Well, the best of luck to you". "Thanks", was accompanied by another great smile. Following a growing pause, "Well, I'll leave you to your first day of putting up with men. Hope to see you soon." "Me, too", was her goodbye.

As I left the store, I was certain that, indeed, I was very impressed with this charming young lady and that I definitely wanted to see her again. This impulse was without the benefit of sufficient time to scope out my reasoning. There was no question that she was very attractive but, at the same time, she was relative young. I guessed that she was in her early twenties. And there I was in my late forties. Apparently, my emotions were dictating my feelings? Was I reacting to the warmth and the friendliness and openness I received from her or was the weight of my familial demands leading me to find an outlet for my emotions? At that point in time it didn't matter; I was determined to see her again, age difference or no age difference, family responsibilities or not.

Unfortunately, I was scheduled to leave for Europe just days after this wonderful shopping experience. And I'd be gone for a month. Chances are she wouldn't remember me. My gosh, is she married. I hadn't bothered to look at her ring finger. Next time.

Shortly after my return, I headed for the store hoping all the way that she would be working. My daughter's asking if she could accompany me to the mall presented a potential problem. Logically, her shopping plans did not include a men's store.

As I made my way into the store, my mind's radar scanned the large room. There she was! Very subtly, I maneuvered around so that, if luck were with me, she would be the one to wait on me. And it worked. As she approached, I greeted her with a cheerful, "Hi, Nancy." It really surprised her. I received a quizzical look in response. Her facial expression signaled she wasn't sure who I was. Things clicked slightly when I reminded her of our having met on her first day of work.

Cocking her head backward slightly, she laughed and said, "Oh my gosh, uh, yes, uh". She was groping for words. While shaking my head and frowning, I jokingly said, "Great, I'll bet you don't even remember my name." She tilted her head backward, closed her eyes and said, "I'm sorry." Quickly I said, "listen, no problem." Then, "Ok, enough of this. It's Roland, now let's get this show on the road. I came to shop, not to toss a quiz at you." Her smile added to the beauty of her face. As inconspicuously as possible I glanced at her ring finger. *No ring! Yeah!*

Similar to my first visit she cheerfully escorted me around the store. The visit was meeting all expectations when, suddenly, I saw my daughter enter the store. *Oh, oh,* was my reaction. I couldn't have Nancy learning about my "secret" life. I looked at my watch and told her that I had to rush off. While looking over my shoulder to track my daughter's movements, I quickly payed for my purchases and offered a quick, stumbling goodbye to Nancy. I hurried to my daughter and ushered her right out of the store. What a look I got from her!

During the months that followed, I visited the store virtually every week.

Very subtly, I learned that Saturdays were the only fixed day she worked. Her school schedule held too many variables. She was working on her bachelor's degree in math at a local university. Her mental skills added oh so nicely to her physical appeal. Needless to say, I was at the store virtually every Saturday.

Naturally, I couldn't very well be in the store and not buy something. I bought clothing of one sort or another that I never wore. My sons and The Salvation Army were the recipients of many of my purchases. At a later point I became so well known in the store that the manager once asked me to help with the annual inventory.

Finally, after many visits to the store, I worked up the nerve to make my move. As casually as possible I mentioned that, because she had to have realized substantial commissions from my purchases, it was only reasonable that she take me out to lunch. It worked! She agreed. Amazing! The obvious age difference didn't seem to bother her. I learned that she was 22-years old; I was 49. Good Lord, I was old enough to be her father! At least to this point she showed no signs that age was an issue. How about me? What were my plans, my intentions? Things were progressing so nicely that I didn't want to ask or know.

She was endowed with so many fine attributes, the manner in which she handled our particular – peculiar? – relationship from day one, certainly was one of them. As our relationship evolved, I really wrestled with the age thing. She was so young. We dated for three years so we got to know each other really well. We were very, very compatible and loved being together. Typically, when we were out, she liked to walk arm in arm. I'll admit that, at first, it felt a little awkward for me. Yes, people "looked" at us, my assumption being that they interpreted our situation as one of an old guy with a young trophy chick, or a young lady with her sugar daddy. Little by little I got used to it and stopped worrying about appearances or other people's opinions. There was absolutely no indication that our age difference bothered her.

It was logical as our relationship grew, that Nancy inquired more and more about my background. This caused problems for me. How was I going to share my complicated life – and prior life – with her? I was afraid that once she learned about my previous marriage and my many children that she would terminate our relationship. Whenever a discussion came close to my living conditions, I opted for a tongue-in-cheek response. I told her I ran a boarding house which, in a way, wasn't too far from the truth. At that point, three of my children were still living with me, two of the others having left for college.

Well, one day Nancy decided to call me at home. This was before cell phones! Looking up my phone number she noticed a "children's number" at the same address, so, out of curiosity, she decided to try that number. Not too surprisingly one of my children answered. My cover was shattered. I was forced to explain my "secret" life.

She now knew the full story; I had been married and had five children, the oldest just a year younger than her. And there I was nearing the half-century mark. If she decided to walk away from this loaded scene I couldn't have blamed her. The manner in which she handled the situation was so impressive. However, I will admit that a question mark popped up in my mind. Here was a set of bizarre elements stacking up in front of her and nothing seemed to bother her. Should I be the one to question this situation? Not for a second. Everything about Nancy was so open, genuine and beautiful. What a very special person I was blessed to have met.

Dating continued and our relationship deepened. In time and, logically, the matter of…"the next step"…began weaving its way into our conversations. The more we talked about it the more guarded I became. During many quiet moments I wrestled with the matter of our ages. It was a nagging problem. Certainly, many men and women of disparate ages had successful marriages. However, I wasn't acquainted with any of these. I had no sounding board or reference manual.

Also, what could I expect down the road? I started playing the numbers' game as well as trying to probe the future. I was now 52. Should we be together for, say, twenty years, I would then be 72; Nancy, 45. Would she look on me as an old man which, of course, I would be. Would she leave me for someone younger? I had already undergone severe emotional trauma in recent years due to a broken marriage. Obviously, this contributed to my fears as well as to one of my troublesome shortcomings — I tried too often to reach too far into the future. I didn't like surprises and, accordingly, tried to anticipate as much as possible. Well, life was wonderful at the moment so why worry about matters I had little or no control over? Besides, there were other good signs that factored in.

From the outset, Nancy seemed to be comfortable enough in meeting and interacting with my daughter and two sons who still lived with me; the other two sons having gone away to universities. For those at home, their acceptance of Nancy didn't occur over night. Once they got around the "old-guy-- young-chick- syndrome", relationships grew steadily. She was so easy to get along with, her having been endowed with a great, and outgoing and non-judgmental personality. This was really gratifying. I'm sure there was plenty of chatting about us in my absence which, of course, was natural.

My mother also factored into the equation. A very old-school lady, having arrived from France in 1919, she never shied away from expressing her opinions. As things became more and more serious between Nancy and me, I mentioned progressively more about our relationship. Initially, I got the predictable earfuls on the age-difference matter. Even though my mother was known for her lectures or "sermons", I valued her judgment and "gut feelings". Prior to marrying my first wife, my mother asked if we weren't hurrying matters a bit. Did I know my wife-to-be well enough? Yes, there was wisdom there.

At a relatively early point, I had my mother come to Sacramento to celebrate her eightieth birthday and, as well, to meet Nancy. I was really nervous. I needn't have been. I had taught Nancy how to say in French…"Happy Birthday Madame Bain, I am very happy to meet you." My mother was thrilled. She produced a happy, hardy laugh at Nancy's accent, Nancy having taken several Spanish courses in high school and college. It was an excellent beginning. As time and events moved forward, the two became very close, in part, because Nancy shared my mother's taste for anything old-school or old-world. Years later when my mother was in care facility near us, Nancy was a frequent visitor.

I remember, at one point, Nancy sharing with me her having asked her mother what she thought of the age difference relative to our marrying. Her mother was a beautifully practical person and, as such, told Nancy to try not to reach too far into the future. As long as Nancy felt that she knew as much as she could about my character and felt that she genuinely loved me, then she should be comfortable about marrying me. To the best of my knowledge, it was the only time I can remember Nancy bringing up the matter of my age.

Like her mother, Nancy's father was so accepting of me and of my relationship with his daughter. Thanks to Nancy and her sister, a comical incident occurred between their father and me. The two insisted that I ask their father for his permission to marry his daughter. Oh my, that's all I needed. They wouldn't let up. It was a half-serious, half- light-hearted insistence. The time came when their father and I were alone. There I was at 52; her father at 55, asking for permission to marry his daughter. Talk about feeling ridiculous. After taking three deep breaths, I told him that his daughters insisted that I ask for his permission. He shook his head, burst out laughing and said, "I can't believe they talked you into this." Sometime during our laughing, he gave me his okay. We became good friends.

I had to think very seriously about my religion as well. Whereas Nancy had no formal religious experience, there I was a life-long Catholic – and a divorced one at that. I knew I couldn't marry in the church. Although she couldn't quite grasp this nor the reason why I had to go to church every Sunday, she respected my religious beliefs. Years later she converted to Catholicism and we were married in the church. This beautiful act on her part allowed me to once again receive the Sacraments. What a grand gesture; what a caring and giving person.

And what about having children? This subject hadn't been touched on to any degree during the courtship. Perhaps it was my fault. Perhaps I wanted to avoid this subject as much as possible because life was too good and, basically, relatively uncomplicated at the time. Perhaps, too, if I were apprehensive about marrying a young woman, the thought of fathering more children brought with it even greater apprehension, this to come home to roost years later. I certainly didn't want to be unfair to Nancy; nevertheless, the thought of again being faced with rearing children – and me at an advanced age – bothered me quite a bit.

Nancy, of course, didn't have the baggage I carried. Logically, she aired a few minor misgivings from time to time about my complicated family life; however, the contents of my background apparently were not of great concern to her.

Prior to marriage, I let each of my children know that Nancy and I planned to be married. Each of them appeared to be comfortable with the announcement, given the fact that we had been dating for over three years.

Well, the marriage took place on the first day of summer in her parent's walnut orchard. It was a wonderful setting and occasion. Each of my children and my mother was there. After a three-week honeymoon in Hawaii we settled into a lovely home that fronted on a large river.

Just prior to our marriage Nancy had received her Master's Degree in math and had been offered a teaching position at a local college.

Also, my consultancy as a petroleum geologist was now robust and very successful. Life was good; we'd worry about the twenty-seven-year age difference some other day.

During the first five years of our marriage we traveled extensively; most of it by car in Europe. We were beholden chiefly to Nancy's school schedule. From time to time my work, in the form of oil or gas drillings projects, overrode travel plans, otherwise we were very fortunate to be able to work traveling around her school schedule and my work. There was no question about it, we led a very privileged life style. Yes, life was good, but it was soon to change.

CHAPTER 3

STARTING A FAMILY

Late one afternoon while Nancy and I were enjoying a glass of wine on our deck, she surprised me with a sudden question: What did I think about starting a family? Oh my, what an immediate internal reaction. I don't know what my outward expression revealed. We had been so privileged thus far to have enjoyed so many of life's pleasures and we really hadn't touched on the subject to any degree during our four years of marriage. Nancy had been busy with her schoolwork and I had been deeply involved in, and please with my work, and we had traveled extensively. Why disrupt this ideal life? Later, during my serious pondering of the relative sudden timing of the question, I had to assume that her sister's having recently started a family played a role in Nancy's thinking process. At one point while discussing the possibility of having children, the matter of her age was brought up. She was now 30. She didn't want to wait much longer.

Children? *Oh Lord, what a scary thought.* I'd been through demanding times in raising and shepherding five children through the highly challenging 1960s and 1970s, and what about my age, now 57? That seemed so old to be starting a family — another family! Adding to my dilemma was the fact that my older brood included twins. The possibility of additional twins? *My goodness, that's all I need.*

My thoughts and possible concerns, of course, extended to my older children. They had no vote in the matter; nevertheless, I wasn't looking to add more confusion to their lives or to cause an estrangement, given what they'd already experienced.

I kept my principle concerns to myself. Yes, I aired certain of my thoughts with Nancy; however, in much the same manner as she had ignored our age difference during the courting stage, she looked upon my fathering another child in a similar manner--age didn't matter. I'm not sure which caused the most reflection, re-marrying or starting a second family. Frightening as the thought was, initially, I reached the bottom line fairly rapidly—I had to be fair to Nancy.

Once the decision was made and Nancy was pregnant, the fun began. Nancy and her sister teamed up to start planning for the great event. What a pair! At an early point I was informed that I'd have to move my office from the house; the room I used would become a nursery. The two of them then planned all the details. Ed was to be a spoiled baby.

Another surprise hit me once the pregnancy was well along, Lamaze classes. *Lamaze? What in the world is that?* I might have heard the name before but had no idea what it meant. To the best of my knowledge, no such thing existed when my older children were born. Once Nancy explained it to me my reaction was, *Oh me, what's next? How am I going to handle this?*

I don't remember how many weeks the classes lasted, but it was an experience I'll never forget. Obviously, Nancy and I weren't the typical couple. I sensed from the looks on the other participants' faces that they might have said, privately, "Oh, how nice that her father is helping her." My feeling out of place came into focus when we got into the "huffing and puffing" exercises. It was a ridiculous endeavor for me at first, but I'll have to admit that I did a pretty good job of it later while coaching her when she was in labor. Her sister, who had attended some of the classes with us, was the superior co-coach.

Even during her pregnancy, we managed to travel. Yes, it was more trying for Nancy, but she coped quite well. One of the trips was to Italy; another to Washington, D.C. followed by a coast-to-coast return train trip. This last trip was just short of three months prior to the due date.

Nancy's labor wasn't an easy one. It started with what became a dry run to the hospital, better known as "false labor". Once labor started in earnest it became a protracted one. We all worked hard. Nancy was exhausted. As her co-coaches we did the best we could. Then came the fun, as her mother, sister and I were invited into the delivery room. That was not what I expected; it was a first for me and I would have just as soon done what I had during the delivery of my older children: pace in the waiting room or in the hallways. At 57, I thought, *Give me back the good ole days.*

Our son Ed was born on the 4th of July, five years after Nancy and I were married. The doctor asked if I would like to cut the umbilical cord. Oh my, what could I say? This was a first for me. With a shaking hand I did, and actually felt good about it.

Ed's arrival resulted in a mere pause in our travel schedule. We let Ed reach the ripe old age of four months before taking him on his first trip, a Caribbean cruise. We flew to Orlando, Florida, where we boarded the ship's shuttle bus. I'll always remember the glances (or were they stares?) we received when we boarded the bus. This was a geological field trip to the western Caribbean; hence the participants and their wives were more or less on the older side. Their faces told the story: What's this old guy doing bringing his daughter and grandson on this cruise? By the time the cruise ended, Ed had been adopted by many aunts and uncles. He proved to be an excellent traveler.

Three years following Ed's birth, Nancy came up with the idea that Ed needed a brother. It shouldn't have come as a surprise, but it did. My knee-jerk reaction was…*WOW!* I had some serious reservations. Wasn't I too old for this? I was 60. What shape would I be in when the boys reached their teens? In Ed's case, I'd be 70. I could only shake my head. When all was said and done, it didn't take long for a decision to be made. Fathering six versus seven children was an irrelevant point. Nancy and Ed had to be considered first and foremost. At least I wouldn't have to attend Lamaze classes this time.

Our son, Scott, joined the family in 1988, during the month of November. Similar to the experience with Ed, Scott was six-months old before we introduced him to traveling. Yes, it was a challenge to venture out with two small children, but Nancy and I decided that our love for travel overrode the consideration of these difficulties.

Ed was about two when I started taking him to church and grocery shopping with me. I don't know how many times people asked me if he were my grandchild. After a while I was tempted to just let it go and answer, yes. However, I reasoned that if I started doing this, it might become confusing for him. When asked, I just produced subtle nod.

Two months following Ed's birth one of my older children fathered a daughter, my first grandchild. Now it got a little complicated: What was the relationship between Ed and my granddaughter? The answer was easy enough; however, it seemed unusual that he had a niece just two months his junior.

Our traveling continued in-step with Nancy's school schedule.

We did the best we could to keep the boys informed of where we were, but I don't think they much cared. Nonetheless, they were excellent travelers. Interestingly, all of the travels with our children preceded the advent of today's child-entertaining electronic devices (laptops, iPads, and so on).

Yes, life was good and remained good until soon after Ed turned four. We were in for a shock and what a shock it was.

CHAPTER 4

Ed Faces Death

Ed was a little over four years old when we noticed that he was becoming thinner and, over a two- or three-day period, he complained about pains along the right side of his abdominal area. His posture when he walked was a strong indication that something was wrong. His crouching forward reminded me of my bout with appendicitis years earlier. I remember not being able to stand up straight because of sharp pains in my abdomen. Off to the pediatrician we went.

After examining Ed, the young French-accented pediatrician had him immediately undergo a sonogram. The technician spent quite a bit of time on the right side of his lower chest area. An occasional, *hmmm,* told us very little, but did pique our curiosity even more. After many minutes she excused herself saying she wanted the doctor to check the findings.

Within minutes the doctor was in the room and was moving the wand around the same area as had the technician. It was easy enough to interpret the look of concern on her face. Once again, several minutes went by. When she was satisfied with her inspection she asked Nancy and me to accompany her to her office. Nancy and I exchanged quizzical glances.

The pediatrician told us that they were unable to detect Ed's right kidney on the sonogram. Something was masking it. She went on to say that it could be a tumor. I can remember a quiver racing across my body. The doctor answered our questions as best she could, each answer containing the logical point that more tests and, very probably, a biopsy were necessary. She was clear, though, about wanting Ed admitted to the hospital immediately.

Two days later, Ed underwent a very lengthy biopsy. After many lab tests, we were informed by the surgeon that Ed had a malignant tumor the size of a cantaloupe that appeared to be connected to his kidney and, worse, to his liver as well. The large mass was described as a *Wilms tumor*. We were shocked when we were told that Wilms tumors usually were deadly. If we hadn't been sitting, I'm sure the news would have knocked us off our feet. After several seconds of stunned silence with the two of us staring at each other, our questions poured out.

We were told that Ed would have to undergo aggressive chemotherapy treatments immediately in order to shrink the tumor. After weeks of that, the tumor and kidney would have to be removed. Life suddenly took an unexpected sharp turn in the wrong direction.

During the next several days he underwent test after test. The problems and deep concerns multiplied. We learned that the cancer had metastasized to his lungs. Not only would he be undergoing chemotherapy, he'd have to undergo the radiation of his chest and abdominal area at the same time.

During this period, the doctors queried us as to any history of cancer in either of our families. There was no known case on Nancy's side. On my side I recounted my father's fight with cancer. In his case it was cancer of the stomach. He died within a year of having been diagnosed. I was fifteen at the time and I will never forget the ugliness of that disease during the last six months of his life, his having been at home until the day before he died. At the time, the early 1940s, chemotherapy and radiation had not yet become normal, standard treatments for cancer. Only surgery and pain medications were available. My father was fifty years old.

The following months were horrific. With Ed at home we would take him to a children's clinic for aggressive chemotherapy to shrink the tumor. Sadly, it was a form of torture. He became so ill following each session that, logically, he did not want to be anywhere near the clinic. This went on for weeks. He also endured simultaneous radiation treatments. Our hearts ached for him. He became skeletal-like and, of course, bald.

They had embedded a Broviac tube in his upper right chest to facilitate in administering the chemicals directly into an artery. The tube had to be flushed each evening at home, a procedure that added to his anxiety and to Nancy and mine as well.

Prior to surgery, Ed became a form of human lab. The hospital was a teaching center and, at the time, there was not a wealth of information regarding Wilms tumors in the health community with the result that there was quite a bit of curiosity about this disease. Logically, medical students were encouraged to feel the large tumor. Given the potential for rupturing it, a "Do-Not-Touch" sign was finally placed at the head of Ed's bed.

The day for surgery finally arrived. A sense of trepidation was in the air. He'd be free of the tumor and his cancer-riddled kidney. Also, we'd learn whether the tumor had invaded his liver. On the other hand, he'd have to go through life with just one kidney. Many before him had done this; nevertheless, it's frightening when it's one of your children experiencing this.

There was a universal sigh of relief when the doctor informed us that Ed's liver was fine; the tumor had pressed against it but had not invaded it. Overall, he had handled the lengthy surgery well. Now, it was back to the chemotherapy and radiation circuit. In particular, his chest would be heavily radiated in order to fight the tumors that had metastasized there.

While Ed was recovering from his surgery at the hospital, one of my daughters-in-law brought him a foot-tall statue of Superman. Superman soon became his hero and was never far from Ed's side for several years. Superman must have been a rescuing hero for many others as well. Suspended from the ceiling at the Medical Center chemotherapy clinic was a figure of Superman.

One of the tangible expressions of generosity, care and respect that Ed received came from the local Make-A-Wish Foundation. A nurse at the Medical Center contacted the Foundation and conveyed the serious medical problems Ed had faced and continued to face. The Foundation, in turn, arranged with The Rotary Club to construct a concrete bike path around our house. What a beautiful example of people giving to, and helping others.

Each day when the Club members were at the house working, there was bald and skinny Ed in his Superman costume. This wonderful gift was memorialized in a picture that appeared in the Sacramento Bee showing a Rotarian helping Ed, in "uniform" of course, christen the fresh concrete with his handprints.

Ed turned five in 1990, on the 4th of July. A few weeks later Kindergarten started. Would he be able to attend? He was still undergoing chemotherapy treatments. Also, he'd be interacting with other children and we had to be cautious of infections. With the doctor's okay, we decided to let him try. It would be an excellent distraction for him. Sadly, it didn't last long. His energy level was too low. He was still quite weak from all he had undergone and was undergoing. Brief as it was, it was a meaningful experience for everyone: students, teachers, parents and, of course, Ed.

We re-enrolled Ed the following semester. His fellow students were, to a point, considerate of his predicament. Unfortunately, there were a few who just had to take advantage of his situation. Bald-headed, skinny Ed was an easy target for bullying. Fortunately, the majority of the students treated him no differently than the others.

Ed's bout with cancer, his surgeries and chemotherapy treatments spanned a period of close to three years. Clearly, it was an extremely demanding, draining and deeply emotional period for all of us. Fortunately, as we eased into the future, we were blessed with what we regarded as a calm period.

Once Ed was declared a "cancer survivor" and, notwithstanding the requirements of school, jobs and everyday family matters, we packed in as much traveling as time, money and, most particularly, Ed's physical condition would allow. The boys became seasoned travelers. They didn't mind the long plane rides or driving long distances. In fact, they enjoyed the roadside picnics in Europe as much as Nancy and I did. The quaint village of Murren, nestled in the Swiss Alps, also became their favorite place to visit. As Nancy and I jokingly threatened them, we would have felt terrible leaving them at home if they didn't want to re-visit Murren. Rare was the trip to Europe that didn't include re-visiting this beautiful region.

As far as Nancy was concerned, living on a river meant fishing. And fish she did. She and her mother, who lived just three houses away, thoroughly enjoyed sitting on our dock in the late afternoon, fishing poles in hand, a thermos of coffee nearby, reviewing the events of the day. Also, once a week the two engaged in another ritual, playing golf. Yes, life was becoming good again.

As relatively calm as this period was, it had its trying moments.

Our youngest son, Scott, may have felt that he also needed some attention. Generally, he was an excellent athlete and, in particular, an exceptionally good soccer player. A problem during his very early years was his more or less constant battle with asthma. However, his continuing need for medications and his dependence on inhalers wasn't able to keep him down. Nor were the broken arms he suffered on two occasions.

Without question, though, the most traumatic event he experienced was a fall from our deck. He was three years old at the time. Racing along the deck he stumbled, fell and slid right under the railing's lower cross-bar, dropping fifteen feet to the ground below, and landing on his stomach. Fortunately, there were several of us close by. Calling 911 was the first order of business, this accompanied by a chorus of yells telling him to lie completely still. Needless to say he was stunned and crying.

The fire-department personnel arrived in quick order and were great in their handling of the situation. Amazingly, he seemed to have suffered no serious damage, as evidenced when the EMRs evaluated him. One would have expected at least a broken bone. A visit to the emergency room confirmed that he had sustained no significant injuries. How lucky can a person be? Scott's parents suffered the greatest injuries, and these in the emotional trauma department.

Of course, his brother and others gave him a relatively low score for his form while flying through the air, much as is done in diving competitions.

This more or less tranquil period, in retrospect, could very easily be labeled as the calm before the storm. I will always remember the turn of the century as a devastating turning point in our lives. There was no way that we could have foreseen the truly hellacious period that awaited us.

CHAPTER 5

THE GATHERING STORM

The word, cancer, is an ugly word and, in many minds, often represents a death knell. And when it invades the bodies of a husband and wife virtually at the same time, the fears and mind-play expand exponentially. So much happened to Nancy and me in a handful of weeks that I can only shake my head and ask, *What the hell is going on here?*

It was my turn first.

The preamble started early in June, 2001, during my annual physical. The doctor mentioned that my Prostate Specific Antigen (PSA) had increased a couple of points during the intervening year. While my PSA had hovered near level one for twenty years or so, it was now at three. The increase alone was not significant. My physician explained that it could have been caused by a combination of age and the density of the long-enlarged prostate gland. I was 73-years-old at the time.

His opinion changed, however, during the manual examination. His "hmmm" was testimony to the rough area he encountered. He immediately recommended I see a urologist. There was no hint of concern in his voice as he said he'd arrange for an appointment. The procedure was normal. Was I concerned? Perhaps. Curious? Of course. But I wasn't knowledgeable enough to know where things could lead. But I was soon to learn.

The procedure was not something a male will soon forget. It was beyond being uncomfortable. A few days after undergoing the biopsy a call from the urologist announced that the results were positive. His comments were delivered in a matter-of-fact manner. His suggestion that both Nancy and I meet with him did register with me. *Why her*, I asked myself? We were to find out. We met with the urologist on June 4.

The urologist taught us a new term – *Gleason Score*. This ranks the degree of seriousness of the cancerous tissues on a scale of 0 to 10. In my case, my score was about 7.5. In the doctor's opinion, this was quite high and indicated a relatively high stage of cancer. Now was the time to be concerned. According to him the usual course of action was to surgically remove the prostate. He did mention that a combination of hormone treatment and radiology was an option. Naturally, my mind started to hunt for ramifications. What does that mean in real terms? The questions stacked up.

Needless to say, Nancy and I had a lot to talk about. The research for the wisest path to follow was underway. The first order of business was to seek a second opinion. The results were worse than the first. The Gleason Score came out between 8 and 9 which, logically, greatly amplified my concern. This confirmed that the cancer was a very aggressive form. One of the chief concerns was whether the cancer had escaped from the gland.

Making a decision was tough. Opinions and/or recommendations from radiologists, other urologists and physicians ran the gamut from surgery to radiation and hormone treatment to the implanting radioactive pellets into the prostate which, at that point, was a relatively new procedure. One radiologist said that prostate surgery was a very difficult procedure, — "Like operating at the base of a funnel." That, of course, did not sit well with me.

If there were a majority opinion, it was for radiation coupled with hormone treatment, and this principally because of my age.

This changed after a visit with a specialist who introduced me to the Partin Table. This measuring method factors in the various key parameters — the Gleason Score, PSA and the estimated clinical stage. The bottom line was that I was at high risk for the spread of the cancer.

In the end, surgery won out.

Thoughts and fears and exaggerations now permeated my mind. Once I knew that cancer had invaded my body it created the fear that I had lost some form of control over what was going on inside of me and there was nothing I, personally, could do about it. It was scary. It was difficult to focus on other matters when I was alone. Fortunately, our two children, Ed (15) and Scott (12) were great distractions. Of course, Nancy was an absolutely great source of support.

The news of June was bad enough. Little did we know what really bad news was. As the opening lyrics of a popular song go, "We've only just begun."

Then it was Nancy's turn.

Virtually one month to the day after learning of the cancer in my prostate, Nancy learned via a biopsy that a lump in her left breast was cancerous. The surprise was that roughly three years earlier a benign lump had been removed from the other breast. During the months prior to the second biopsy, Nancy had been aware of the lump becoming larger to the point that her growing concern prompted her to make an appointment with her primary physician. A mammogram led to an echogram which, in turn, led to a biopsy. Oh, so sadly, the tumor was malignant, the stage of the cancer at a very high level. This was a double whammy. It was July 5, 2001.

As soon as the biopsy's pathology report was available she was referred to a surgeon. If there were any good news associated with this ordeal it was that the surgeon was young and handsome. Both Nancy and her sister were in complete agreement on this point. Unfortunately, that was the only positive news.

In addition to the stress she experienced in knowing that the lump was growing and that it was cancerous, she was tired quite a bit of the time and had fairly frequent headaches. Also, her knees and shoulders ached much of the time. Accordingly, the doctor ordered a full- body scan as well as a CT scan of her chest area.

Whereas I, in a sense, had a couple of options, Nancy was limited to one – surgery, and surgery at the earliest possible date. The urgency aside, we both engaged in a lot of research on the respective subjects. We also engaged in quite a few discussions with friends who had, or who knew someone who had faced similar challenges. Though normal, this exercise changed nothing.

I had been scheduled for surgery on July 7; however, because of the urgency of Nancy's situation, my surgery was postponed until the following month. This allowed us to focus on Nancy. Needless to say, fears and frustration reigned.

The balancing act between mental and practical preparations for the surgeries, and caring for children and professional matters, was something else again. Thank the Lord for the great support from our family and friends.

So, Nancy went first. About six weeks after the biopsy report, she underwent surgery to remove the lump. Nancy's mother, sister and I were very nervous. Added to that was a longer-than-expected wait. Because the surgical procedure was not terribly complicated, which we felt was in Nancy's favor, we expected a reasonably early report from the doctor.

Not so. Time dragged on and the nerves remained taut. At long last the doctor asked us to join him in the hallway. His face bore no smile. After letting us know that Nancy had handled the procedure well, he went on to say that the cancerous mass was much larger than expected. Also, he was very concerned about the "margins" around the tumor. They were not "clean." The cancer covered more area than had been anticipated. Interestingly, neither the mammogram nor the CT scan defined the large size of the mass.

The surgeon's counsel was that Nancy undergo an immediate and complete mastectomy of the affected breast. Because there were no alternatives it was, in a sense, an easy decision.

How absolutely sad for Nancy. When we were able to see her in her room, the expression on her face testified to the uncertainty and helplessness and internal turmoil she had to be experiencing. Her eyes scanned each of us searching for help or a solution. The surgery was scheduled for the next day.

It was so difficult to explain to the boys just was going on. It was a balancing act between letting them know enough about the severity of their mother's medical issues, but not enough to overly frighten them. I felt so sorry for them. They were aware that I, too, had a serious enough problem that required surgery. The beautiful support from grandparents, aunts and uncles and friends kept the boys busy and distracted.

The following morning — really, the entire day — will always stay with me. It started with my wheeling Nancy to the double doors that separated the medical world from the outside world. During the brief wait for an attendant I did what I could to keep her spirits up. The attendant attempted to lighten the mood with quick-witted comments. It helped a little. Nancy and I kissed and said our goodbyes.

What can be said at a time like that? I could see the fear in her eyes despite the brave appearance she tried so hard to maintain. The fellow wheeled her into the operating-room area. It was a terrifically sad and deeply emotional moment. She looked so alone; so forlorn. I projected my own fears and fright into what I imagined she was experiencing. I hated that moment. I leaned against the wall and cried. The fear that she might not make it through the surgery invaded my mind. Back-to-back surgeries would be rough. But she was a very strong individual. She'd make it; she had to.

Many agonizing hours passed before the surgeon came out. It was a session I gladly would have missed. He described the results of the surgery and mentioned that Nancy handled it well. The worst part of his comments focused on the fact that the cancer had spread into many of the neighboring lymph nodes.

The negative report hit each of us harder than expected. It was an ugly outcome. The very kindly surgeon did his best to convey encouragement. Her case would be transferred to an oncologist/hematologist and he felt confident that chemotherapy would arrest the cancer's progress. Hopefully, the combination of chemotherapy and radiation, should rid her of this horrible disease.

Needless to say, he offered no guarantees. Co-mingled with my attempt to digest his words was my concern about how I was going to be able to maintain a positive composure when I saw her again. After the surgeon left, the three of us hugged and cried. We were able to see her once she was in her room. The surgeon had already told her the results of the surgery and the related pathology report. She cried when she saw us and after some solid hugging and kissing, she produced at least half a smile and said, "Some kinda news, huh?".

Why her? I asked again and again? And this without really understanding what lay ahead. Oh, boy, if we'd only known what lay ahead. The mind games that had to be at play within her, just had to be something else. I had to ask, *"Why her? Why not me?"*

Here was this truly genuine, lovely and giving person, one who possessed a beautifully charitable heart, being confronted by who knew what. Really, so often I told people that I would have loved to have had her Christian outlook and attitude. She wasn't religious in the formal sense but she was such a giving and non-judgmental person. Her attitude was always so positive. You just felt good when in her presence.

The impact of what their mother now faced would have on our children raced around my mind. I cried just thinking about it. I would have to script my words carefully to convey this news as gently as possible and with the lowest level of negativity possible.

On the one hand, leaving the hospital was a good step forward for Nancy. On the other, the uncertainties of the future overshadowed any positive feelings. It was so very difficult to grasp just what the near future held in store for her; and really, for all of us. The weeks and months ahead would hold much more than any one of us could have imagined.

CHAPTER 6

LEAP-FROG SURGERIES

Then it was my turn.

It seemed like Nancy and I were developing a leap-frog pattern for our ailments, treatments and surgeries, first one of us, then the other.

Nancy's surgeries, nightmarish as they were, served to distract me from my issues, at least temporarily. Now I had to focus on my turn in the operating room. No one wants to undergo major surgery, regardless of the seriousness of the problem. I was both apprehensive and afraid. Here I was at seventy-three years old, going under the knife. Even with the doctor's assurance that I would have no problem, the age thing did bother me.

Nancy and our boys were at my bedside in the prep room. This added to my fears. Would I see them again? How would they cope if I didn't come out of this, particularly considering Nancy's condition? Obviously, I was going through the expected mental and emotional machinations. And there was Nancy, one month after her surgery, concerned with my problem. Bless her; she was so good at keeping the atmosphere light and cheerful.

Interestingly, what troubled me quite a bit was in knowing I would have a catheter for a week after surgery. I had never had one before and the idea bugged me, even though I would be unconscious while the tube was inserted. This concern all but overrode my dreading the possibility of ending up incontinent. Once again, strange is the imagination.

The surgery went well. The urologist was pleased that the area around the prostate appeared to be free of cancerous tissues and that the lymph nodes also were clear. Catheter or not, that was great news. I had entered the operating room feeling certain the cancer had escaped the gland.

I was pleased, too, that each of my older children and several of my grandchildren visited me during my three-day stay in the hospital. Nancy, simultaneously, was undergoing a series of scans; still, she was there each day to see me. She was like a ray of sunlight. Ed and Scott came with her when they could. They gave the appearance of having their fill of hospitals.

A few days after I returned home, Nancy started chemotherapy. It was now late 2001. The protocol spanned twelve weeks, with a heavy-duty treatment administered every three weeks.

It saddened me not to be with her as she embarked on this uncertain path. It was still difficult for me to move around with that miserable catheter still with me. Fortunately, her sister was staying with us. This was a decided plus because of her upbeat personality. Smiles and cheerfulness characterized her.

Nancy realized at the outset that what she was going to have to go through was not going to be pleasant. For whatever reason, she had to have an intravenous connection on the back of her hand for each treatment. The veins along the backs of her hands were so small that inserting the needle was difficult. Typically, more than one attempt was necessary. She dreaded this more than the treatments and, more than once, she came close to fainting.

The impact of September 1, 2011 (9/11) overrode any of our personal concerns. What a devastating event. For days afterward, we attended to our individual medical needs in a perfunctory manner. Our focus was on our country. During the balance of September and through the month of October, Nancy's treatments occupied center stage. Chemotherapy, losing her hair, low blood counts, continuing to teach math at her college, being a mother and generally feeling rotten filled her days and weeks. It was not a pleasant period. Who wouldn't be impressed with how she coped? What a strong person. Another unfortunate manifestation of the chemicals was in the weight gain. Sadly, it manifested itself most noticeably around her face. Crying spells were frequent; nevertheless, she strove to maintain a positive attitude for the kids' sake.

In fact, she infused her situation with frequent touches of humor. She was now able to play golf, but only one round a week. On one of the outings, she teamed up with a neighbor. Once the pair had left the first tee, Nancy removed her wig and placed it on a plastic "head" she carried with her. She told the neighbor she wasn't about to let the club members see her bald. The wig was back in place well before they reached the eighteenth green.

Given all that was coming at Nancy, one would think that her mood would be dark and despondent. Not so. I don't know how she did it but during our afternoon respites on the deck, she often led our chats away from medical problems to focus instead on matters concerning our children or my work, or about her teaching or that she had to get busy in her garden. Sure, we shed tears often enough; however, I can't remember her at any time wallowing in self-pity. How many times I wished for just half of her brave attitude.

And Nancy would need as much of that positive attitude as she could muster for the coming weeks. That said, and perhaps beneficially, her woes once again were sidelined in deference to my own worries, coming in the "what-else-can-happen" department.

The answer came…it was my turn again.

During the weeks that followed our surgical ordeals, I became increasingly aware of a growing problem with my left eye. When I tried to focus while reading, the letters of the words in the center of my vision became distorted. The distortions grew as the weeks passed. An ophthalmologist found a hole in the macular area of my retina. Left unattended, the hole would widen and my vision in that eye would deteriorate greatly leading to near blindness. And the remedy was really something. As it turned out, the surgery on my eye was the easy part.

Unfortunately, the surgery was scheduled on Scott's thirteenth birthday. It was a window of opportunity for the doctor, a specialist in this type of surgery, so I had to take advantage of it. The procedure consisted of draining the gel from that eye and replacing it with a particular type of gas. Again, that was the easy part. For the next seven days, I had to keep my face looking down. In other words, I had to look at my feet or lie face down for an entire week. This, of course, required special equipment. For sleeping, I rented a massage table with an opening at one end into which I placed my face. Trying to sleep like this was not easy or pleasant. There was no way to turn over. I dreaded seeing the sun go down.

Another contraption allowed me to lean forward and rest my forehead on a padded cross-bar. This allowed me to watch a portable television set propped up on its end on the floor. Trying to keep food in my mouth was one of many frustrations. Another was the teasing I got from the boys as I walked around head down. It was a very long week.

Roughly three months went by before the bubble in my eye completely disappeared. Even at that point, my vision was quite blurry. I was told during one of the follow-up appointments that I would need cataract surgery in about six months. As predicted, I underwent cataract surgery six months later.

Meanwhile, Nancy was fighting the rigors of chemotherapy. During the latter part of November, she entered another phase. At this point in time she went in for a treatment every week. To her credit, she continued to teach throughout the many weeks of physical and emotional hardships. In a sense, it was a form of medication. I wanted her to continue teaching as long as it didn't tire her too much. There were concerns, too, about her driving but she seemed to manage everything well enough.

Due to the efforts of her parents, her sister, a neighbor friend and, of course, Nancy, we had dinners that were easy for the boys to prepare, during the time when I was incapacitated. However, if I had one concern during this period, it was being alone with the boys. I wouldn't have been much good to anyone in the event of an emergency. Knowing her parents were nearby helped considerably.

The early part of December was relatively quiet. Besides teaching and trips to the cancer center, Nancy somehow found the energy and drive to plan for Christmas. Early in the month, the thought of the two of us taking a trip — a significant trip—gained increasing appeal. We were exhausted. We were desperate for a break. There had been no traveling for months; not since the illnesses had invaded our bodies. Because school vacations extended from mid-December through mid-January, a get-away seemed like a good idea. When I posed the question to the doctor, though, I received a lukewarm response. Initially, her position was that any lengthy travel would be difficult for Nancy.

When I mentioned that I was considering a resort on the Mediterranean in the south of France, her eyebrows shot up and her mouth opened. After I added that a family member would accompany us and that we would fly first class (neither of which was in place at this point), she waffled. The doctor acknowledged that Nancy would have finished the current round of chemotherapy by then and that the decision really should be up to her. Clearly, though, the doctor was not a strong supporter.

In retrospect, I should have been suspicious of the doctor leaving the decision to Nancy even though she'd been very protective of her patient. It led me to ask myself if the doctor were shielding us from something. Was Nancy's condition worse than we thought? Or was it because of Nancy's increasing fatigue and malaise? Was she telling us that we might as well try such an endeavor while Nancy could still move around?

Throughout our relationship with her, the oncologist had been forthright and positive. Always a caring person, she treated each negative episode in a matter-of-fact way but always leading us to believe that Nancy's chances of clearing each hurdle were good. We thought she would clear this one as well.

The idea of traveling injected a strong dose of positive energy and enthusiasm into Nancy. Once again it was fun to put together the nuts and bolts of a trip.

Sadly, we didn't get too far. The high didn't last long. Little by little, Nancy realized, logically, that she just wouldn't be able to handle the mechanics of a trip. In addition to her considerable pain and discomfort, her concerns grew over the possibility of a serious problem arising while we were in a foreign country. We were operating in a desperate mode. Disappointment and reality teamed up to lead us to cancel travel plans.

I was impressed that Nancy didn't dwell on the matter. The brief planning period certainly was a needed distraction. Yes, she expressed regrets, but those were soon replaced by her very direct attitude. "By gosh," she said. "If we can't travel then we'll find another way to have a great Christmas."

During the weeks and days prior to Christmas, Nancy complained of vision problems in her left eye as well as an increasing frequency of headaches and backaches. Nevertheless, with the support of the combined families and our many friends, the holidays were wonderful indeed. The flow of people during the days before and after Christmas was excellent medicine for Nancy; it was a happy distraction. The pain, always there, seemed more tolerable during this period.

We couldn't wait for 2001 to end. It had been one hell of a year. However, little did we know what the New Year held in store for Nancy; really, for all of us. She was about to enter a very ugly period of rapidly moving developments.

CHAPTER 7

CANCER SPREADS RAPIDLY GRASPING FOR MIRACLES

A brand new year had no sooner opened than Nancy's increasing pain sent us back to the oncologist's office. The first order of business was an MRI. The results were not good. The neuro-oncologist and radiologist detected a tumor in the *pons* area at the base of her brain (the brain stem). To deepen the trauma, a contrast MRI indicated ten or twelve small tumors across her brain. Answers to our ongoing rhetorical question, "What's next?" were forthcoming.

What followed was a case in which the treatment was worse than the malady. It was almost inhumane. The procedure used to deal with her brain-stem tumor is called "Gamma-knife surgery". A heavy metal frame is attached to the skull with screws. What punishment! It was terribly painful for her. It also was terrible to see her that way. When her sister and I first saw her with that contraption screwed to her head it was impossible not to cry. But brave Nancy's first words were, "Roland, you'd never make it through this." It put a weak smile on our faces.

It was difficult watching her being wheeled away. Perhaps it wasn't as sad a sight as her having been wheeled away for her mastectomy; nonetheless, it hit me hard.

Inside the treatment room, the frame was bolted to a receptacle within a huge concave, hemispheric device that contained a number of nozzle-like ports. Radiation rays were generated at the ports and beamed to focus on the pons-area tumor. Fortunately, this part of the treatment was painless—except for the deep emotional pain. Of course, her skull hurt for several days. It was terrible to see the points at which the frame had been attached.

No matter how poorly things were going, Nancy somehow managed to rise above the never-ending bad news. In a letter to family and friends she described her situation. After commenting on the problems I'd had, she went on to write:

> *The newest and most disturbing news has added another trauma to my life; we've just found out that this darn cancer has spread to my brain and is affecting my eyesight. But even with this disturbing news, there's still a silver lining. The newest treatment for brain tumors is called gamma knife surgery. It really isn't surgery. It's a heavy dosage of radiation aimed at the tumor. It has a very good success rate and a near-zero mortality rate, so it's no longer the death sentence it used to be. Other than our unusual health issues, things are really pretty good around here.*

Characteristic of Nancy's resiliency was her great capacity to rebound. You could knock her down but she'd bounce right back.

Ten days after the gamma knife treatment she commenced a three-week session of radiation on her head called whole-brain radiation. Twelve of these treatments spanned the rest of January. During this period came more CT and bone scans as well. Nancy was exhausted but that didn't stop her from heading right back to the school room when the new semester started.

Toward the end of January, the doctor hit Nancy with another bombshell: The scans indicated that the cancer had invaded many more lymph nodes, and worse, her liver. When would the devastating news stop—or would it? The doctor also informed her that she was being dropped from the clinical trials due to the elevation of the cancer stage from three to four.

Although it was becoming difficult to find anything to be positive about, Nancy's spirits somehow remained reasonably high. Mine didn't. I was caught up in the adage that, once the liver was involved, the word, *terminal,* was virtually synonymous. This was in part due to how the doctor conveyed this information to Nancy. At no time did her voice or words carry any degree of finality. Whatever the next report of bad news might have brought, a positive tone was always tied to the treatment. We always felt that we were made aware of the important facts. It was easy enough to grasp the severity of Nancy's condition.

The doctor's positive approach was reflected in her descriptions of the next round of chemotherapy. This time it would be in the form of tablets, a relatively new form of chemotherapy. Several days later, Nancy commenced the new round of chemotherapy. In whatever shape or form the ongoing procedures came, they continued to offer her a ray of hope. It seemed as though each new negative pronouncement resulted in an increased volume of prayer. During this period I, a lifelong Catholic, was frequently kneeling in a chapel pleading for help, for a miracle. As the cancer continued its invasion of her body and brain, matters concerning God and life and death became increasingly important to all of us.

Praying, of course, was an outlet and I did a lot of it. Often enough I wept in the quiet of the chapel. Otherwise, the only venue for my tears was on the phone with a dear friend who lived in Corona del Mar.

Paul was my sounding board, listening ear, counselor and soul brother. We'd been members of the Beta Theta Pi fraternity at UCLA and had maintained close contact across the intervening years. How many times did he hear me sob on the phone? Certainly, I kept my local friends and associates informed and they saw tears form more than once, but I somehow held off from completely breaking down. I'm not sure why, but it seems as though adult males are reluctant to cry in front of other adult males. Because I didn't want to show emotions in front of Nancy, at least no more than necessary, I needed an outlet other than church and Paul was it.

Nancy, on the other hand, shared her troubles, often in the form of crying, and mainly with her sister and her mother. It was so good that she had these loved ones nearby. Yes, she had tears from time to time in front of the boys; however, she kept that at a minimum. As the post-Christmas events unfolded, she shared more details with them but always very deftly.

Both of us answered their questions in the most uplifting manner possible. There was no need to go into a lot of detail. Obviously, their curiosity rose with changes in her appearance and the chatter they picked up during our conversations with others. It pains me now to picture the quizzical and slightly frightened look on their faces. Oh, how deeply sorry I was for them. Without question, we were all frightened. Nancy, of course, had to be experiencing emotions and fears that none of us could imagine.

During a phone conversation with the wife of my close friend Paul, I learned of a saint whose name was unfamiliar to me, Saint Peregrine. He was regarded as the *"cancer Saint"*. Our prayers immediately were directed to this Thirteenth Century saint. At a Catholic store, I bought a medal of Saint Peregrine for Nancy. She wore it around her neck. We continued to be in a strong reaching-out mode.

As we soon learned, saints are not just from another age or religiously connected; they are in our daily lives and operate in different ways.

Even in the midst of the persistent and increasing flow of disheartening news, one aspect of this saga stood out—the incredible support from family, neighbors and friends. It started early in 2002, and was unexpected.

Our next-door neighbor initiated the "guardian-angel" pilgrimage. Without fail, every Monday afternoon she was at our door with that evening's dinner. It was a beautiful act of compassion. As it became increasingly difficult for Nancy to perform regular chores, the neighbor's gift of goodwill became even more important.

One of the most moving displays of caring and contribution came from the charter school our son, Scott, attended. By definition, these schools have smaller enrollments than regular middle schools. Accordingly, the teaching staff is much smaller. Once it became too difficult and dangerous for Nancy to drive herself to school, several of the teachers worked up a schedule and took turns driving Nancy to work. Talk about heart-warming! Talk about saints!

One of her "designated drivers" showed me a neatly organized, typed schedule. It was amazing. From time to time the driver also delivered a prepared meal. A little humor went along with this. The physical education teacher, one of the few male teachers there and a very eligible bachelor, volunteered to furnish a dinner. The other teachers were very curious about his cooking skills, if any. His enchilada casserole was a winner and, once the word spread, his popularity increased accordingly.

If these beautiful people couldn't prepare dinner for us, then meals were left up to me. It was no contest. Ed and Scott couldn't wait for meals from neighbors or the" Angeles" to arrive. I tried to keep my ego in check.

Getting Nancy to school was one thing; getting her home late in the evening was another. One of the charter school teachers who lived a short distance from the college occasionally delivered Nancy to school and brought her home later. Otherwise the chauffeur duties were handled by Nancy's mother and sister, other family members and me.

This chapter of Nancy's life clearly demonstrated the genuine beauty in life, the giving and caring—with no expectation of reward—we don't hear about often enough. I refer to them as the "beautiful People". Co-mingled with this caring was an unspoken, ominous sense that Nancy's deterioration was gathering momentum. Her appearance, in particular her face, testified to the changes. Perhaps these manifestations influenced others to help. The fact that in her deteriorating condition, she could continue to teach was a great testimony to her strength of character.

Whereas the company of our two sons was her main source of emotional sustenance, teaching was a close second. She absolutely loved teaching math. Her appearance didn't trouble her a bit. At one point, she would arrive in her class room, oxygen tank in tow, wearing a patch over one eye and her cute bonnet. She was truly an incredible person.

One evening she arrived home from the college beaming from ear to ear. She had just taught a class in calculus. Her early words were: "I was sooo good tonight. They really understood what I was conveying. No one went to sleep. They paid attention and grasped the concepts I taught. I could tell from their faces and questions." The comment she made was not born of pride, but one of deep satisfaction.

One of the interesting aspects of this seven-month experience was that part of the time we wanted to be realistic and admit we were losing the battle, while at other times we remained hopeful and in denial. We glided from treatment to treatment without looking too far into the future. It was a day-to-day routine. We became so focused on looking for positive results from whatever treatment was at hand that perhaps we weren't seeing the bigger picture. In a sense it was an inability to see the forest for the trees.

Without question, the element of fear hovered in the backs of our minds, but it had not yet been put into words. We never felt that key information was being withheld, but the ongoing, never-ending series of blows kept us off balance. True, the doctors frequently just didn't know what might be around the next corner. Perhaps not knowing every outcome allows people to continue to hope for positive news.

The news that came at us early in February fell right in with the parade of bad news that had shadowed Nancy for so long. A meeting with the oncologist on the last day of January set the tone for February, and it was a miserable one.

CHAPTER 8

Nancy's Condition Worsens Yet She Continues to Teach

Nancy's vision, particularly in her left eye, had been troubling her for several weeks. The worsening of this condition led her to see an ophthalmologist early in February. Not the least bit surprising was the news that a tumor had formed in her left eye. Another hit on the emotional center.

This new development in no way deterred Nancy from teaching. With a patch over her eye, she plowed right on with her passion. Her students and fellow teachers were so warm-hearted in their treatment of her without qualification. Being able to teach math in a variety of forms may have been the best medicine. Yes, it was awkward for her to function with only one eye; nevertheless, this was her crusade. The only requirement was for the "angels" to get her to and from school then leave the rest to her. Yes, she would come home exhausted, but that didn't matter; she would not abandon her students.

As the month progressed, Nancy experienced more and more chest and back pain. Suspecting blood clots, the doctor had Nancy undergo a battery of tests; a CT scan of her chest, an echogram of her heart, a sonogram of her legs, and MRIs of her brain and back. It seemed as though she had one of every kind of scan or *gram* the medical world had to offer. During the hospital stay, she started radiation treatments on her back. Returning home a week later, she began the second round of chemotherapy pills.

The days of February were analogous to watching a macabre three-ring circus. Events happened so fast and seemingly came at her from all directions. We were kept off balance. Poor Nancy; all she could do was suffer. Pain was her constant companion. One would think that everything her battered body and mind had suffered would defeat her or cause her to become bedridden. Not so. The determination that woman possessed was amazing.

During this stressful period, it was so difficult to know how our sons were coping. They were in school most of the weekdays, which was good for everyone. Otherwise, it seemed that they spent progressively more time at friends' homes. I couldn't blame them. I did notice when they were at home they did more activities together, such as swimming in the river or playing catch in the backyard. As often as possible the three of us would throw a football or kick a soccer ball around. It was clear that they enjoyed having me team up with them. Often, they'd chide me because I wasn't as "cool" as I should have been. What did they expect from a seventy-three-year-old? Actually, I thought I kept up with them admirably.

There was no avoiding the continuing bad news in our home. As best I could, I tried to inform the boys on what was going on. Their mother being rushed to the doctor's office, hospital or to the emergency room, needless to say, was bewildering to them; really, to all of us. As usual, the details were minimized. She just needed to see the doctor or to be scanned or she had a bad reaction to a certain medication were our typical comments intended to explain the increasing reasons for our hurrying off. Typically, there was little reaction from the boys. If anything, it seemed as though they would look down or away, at least when I tried to give them an update or engage them in conversation. Instead, they just listened. At thirteen and sixteen, how were they supposed to act or react or even know what to say or ask?

However, on the basis of what these very young minds had been exposed to, I would not have been surprised if one of them had asked, *"Is mom dying?"* The subject just had not been broached. It was an unwelcome topic. At the same time, their mother was obviously in terrible pain and her physical appearance had changed dramatically. Whereas she was completely aware of her puffy face and bald head, her demeanor spoke otherwise. Her ability to be cheerful, particularly in front of the boys, was so admirable. It was painful for me to think about what our children were experiencing. I remember well the fear I experienced watching my father die when I was fifteen. The memory of his having suffered terribly during the last six months of his life is tattooed in my mind.

Were we reaching the point at which we'd have to alter our approach to what was confronting us? I can't remember anyone volunteering to venture into that territory.

Whenever and wherever possible, we made adjustments to keep Nancy as comfortable as we could. One adjustment had to do with our bed. Our water bed was comfortable but any movement created waves. I started sleeping on the couch in the living room to let Nancy have the best sleep possible. Rested or not, reliably she was up every week-day morning to make breakfast for the boys and prepare their school lunches. Like teaching, that was her territory, and she wasn't giving it up.

We also started taking short walks in the evening. As difficult as it could be, she enjoyed getting out and it was good for her. Whenever we encountered a neighbor, we'd stop and chat for few moments. If Nancy were embarrassed by her appearance, it didn't show. Actually, she looked rather cute wearing her pill-box hat. The topic of her condition was always avoided. When the boys joined us, it must have made an interesting sight, the four of us slowly walking arm-in-arm along the street.

Nancy's level of stability wasn't the greatest. She leaned heavily on my arm. Once in a while a bob or weave on her part would bring a chuckle from her. "Guess I'd better cut back on the drinking." Per force, she had given up any form of alcoholic beverage long ago. For the most part I was reluctant to delve into the details of how she was feeling. Unless we had to discuss some specific medical procedure, our topics ranged from schedules or events for the boys or her teaching or how nice someone's garden was, or we said nothing. Gradually, the walks became shorter and shorter.

Important, also, were the coffee breaks at her parents' house. It was a short walk to their house, which was great. She and her mother were soul buddies. Nancy could share anything and everything with her mother. She needed that essential outlet. Her mother was of Swiss stock and had a matter-of-fact strength about her. She was a pillar of strength for Nancy. The same can be said about Nancy's sister.

Certainly, Nancy would confide in me and share emotions with me; however, her closeness with her mother and sister was special. I've often pondered the ease women have in sharing deep feelings with one another, whereas men are not similarly inclined. Many men reach some intangible barrier that prevents them from divulging their emotions.

Our prayers and entreaties to God and various saints continued in high gear. Tears became a normal part of praying. My petitions were aimed at obtaining a miracle for Nancy and finding a way to ease her pain. What bothered me most was the feeling that my prayers were falling on deaf ears. During recent weeks and months, Nancy's condition had steadily deteriorated. Why weren't our prayers being answered? It was a troubling emotional struggle.

During late February and early March, Nancy began having difficulty breathing. Also, the pain across her back grew in intensity. Twelve days after the last visit to the hospital, the doctor had her re-admitted. An x-ray showed fluid between her right lung and the chest wall. Draining the chest cavity relieved much of the pain. Predictably, more bad news was announced; an MRI showed that the lesions on her liver were larger and more lymph nodes had been invaded by cancer.

While in the hospital, she received the last of the current round of chemotherapy pills. I brought her home after three days, this time with a portable oxygen tank. She depended on oxygen around the clock. Also, the doctor supplied her with morphine patches and longer-lasting pain pills.

Nancy's spirits somehow remained relatively high. Not for a second did she consider giving up teaching. No sir, her students needed her. It was a sight to behold whenever one of the angels took her to school. We'd put her oxygen tank in the car and away they'd go. What determination! In addition, her students are to be commended for the respect and consideration they gave their teacher.

Five days after her last hospital stay, the pain in her chest was such that I took her to the out-patient wing to have her lungs drained. She was given much stronger morphine patches. That was on a Monday.

It seemed each day brought with it a new symptom or a new pain in a different part of Nancy's body. Some days it felt like we had descended into a robotic lifestyle. She was becoming a regular at the hospital. We were on a first-name basis with many on the staff. Otherwise, we were operating from deep, raw frustration and fear. These feelings were to deepen even more.

As March opened, I faxed the oncologist with growing frequency. These missives carried questions and updates and sought guidance. Rather than facing the frustration of trying to locate the oncologist via telephone, faxing allowed her to digest my queries in a more measured manner.

> *"Dear Dr. Smith: Sorry to keep bothering you but I have two or three questions.*
> *…It has been established that there is a tumor in Nancy's left eye but nothing has been said about its continued growth. In other words, is it expected to continue to grow?*
> *…Nancy has been experiencing quite a bit of back pain. Massaging seems to help. Does the Center offer a massage service?*
> *…With regard to her left breast area, could a dermatologist contribute to an understanding of the rash?"*

The good doctor responded as quickly as her work permitted.

During this period, someone brought up the matter of a Catholic organization, The Knights of Columbus, and the pilgrimages they organized to travel to Lourdes in the south of France. I had visited Lourdes on two occasions and was well-acquainted with the story of Bernadette Soubirou (St. Bernadette) and the 1854 Apparitions of the Virgin Mary. This was the well-known site of many miraculous healings attributed to the Virgin Mary and the miraculous waters. At this point I felt a strong desire to take Nancy to Lourdes.

Predictably, Nancy joined right in with my wishes. She was anxious to make this happen. Naïve on our part? Yes, I'm sure it was. But we were desperate for a miracle.

After several discussions with the Knights of Columbus people in San Francisco, the time came to make a connection between Nancy's doctor and the Knights. Sadly, but not surprisingly, they made the decision that any such trip would be far too difficult for her. The Knights did not want to accept the responsibility. We'd just have to find a miracle somewhere else.

We decided to try a less-demanding trip to Maui. We could stay at my son's house. On March 7, I faxed the doctor:

> *"You asked about Lourdes, France. Unfortunately, Nancy was not accepted as one of the 'Malades' to be included in the Bay Area group that will charter-flight to Lourdes early in May. Given her current condition, they feel that the trip would do more harm than good. I haven't given up yet. I'm looking at other options. Needless to say, yours will be the final say (beyond Nancy's, of course). I haven't told Nancy about the rejection. I'm waiting to hear from them officially. Again, thank you for your gentle and considerate ways."*

On March 14, I faxed the following:

> *"...Nancy was not breathing terribly well this morning when she got up. She calmed down once she took the medication. Just talked to her on the phone and she sounds slightly hoarse and/or congested.*
>
> *...I'm not holding my breath re. Hawaii trip. It's 100% up to her.*
>
> *...The airline will accommodate her needs for oxygen.*

Both a prescription and a flow rate are required (the latter to determine how many bottles will be included).

…Nancy has not brought up the matter of more chemo (or any other approach to attempt to arrest the spread), but the fact that she is not taking anything else these days is troubling. In view of the already-documented spread I just wish there were something that could be done during the next two weeks (even Xeloda, which she tolerates reasonably well). If we cancel Hawaii, will she be able to start another medication right away?

…As you can appreciate, it is so difficult to watch her suffer and to be aware of the fear that must permeate her thoughts. It appears that we are at a point that would open the door to the most aggressive type of treatment possible. It's easy for me to ignore side-effects and the like, but the frustrations that go with all of this dictate more than just positive or assertive attitudes. You'll have to bear with me when I approach you with my frustrations, fears and hopes. If anything out there holds any degree of hope, please consider it."

The month of March was notable because seven family members, including me, had birthdays that month. For several years the tradition had been to throw a collective party. The date was linked to my birthday because it was more or less in the middle of everyone else's dates. It was unclear how we were going to handle the matter that year.

The wheels had been turning in Nancy's mind. She wouldn't hear of letting the occasion go by without some form of recognition or celebration. Accordingly, she took it upon herself to arrange for eighteen of us to take over a small room in a nearby restaurant on my day, Tuesday the 19th; my seventy-fourth birthday.

The morning of the party was not a good one. Nausea and vomiting kept her in bed. As the day progressed her condition improved until she felt strong enough to attend the party. So, off we went with her oxygen tank at her side.

It turned out to be a wonderful event. She had a fantastic time, although, clearly, it was very demanding of her. There was no talk of cancer, scans, or the hospital. Indeed, an exhausting but happy outing for Nancy and, of course, for me.

Off went another fax on Friday, March 22:

> *"Dear Dr. Smith: This is an update and/or progress report.*
>
> *…We saw you on Monday.*
>
> *…Wednesday (Mar. 20) opened with a great deal of pain and the three of us talked about changing the pain medication. She started Oxycontin that evening (the 75 mg patches came off four hours later at midnight).*
>
> *…Thursday (Mar.21) a.m. was terrible; characterized by considerable moaning, panting and just plain hurting. Also, slurring of the words and confusion appeared. She took very little morphine sulfate this day and I'm not sure why. I have taken over dosing her medicine. She went to school in a slightly wobbly albeit very determined state but was home an hour early. School is out next week. She was quite tired the rest of the evening. Her food intake for the day was minimal; some nausea associated. Food just does not interest her.*
>
> *…Friday (Mar. 22) a.m. was reasonably peaceful and restful (although she has not been able to sleep the past two mornings, up at 5:30). I did have her take the morphine liquid. I'm encouraging her to move around as best she can and to inflate her lungs as gently and slowly as she can tolerate.*

> *In short, she was noticeably calmer this a.m. than yesterday. We'll be visiting you on Monday. Your words on the phone the other day were not encouraging re. additional chemo. We just can't give up yet. I hope there is some way to maximize any opportunity for stabilizing her condition. As cruel and disastrous as this time has been, to date, we remain as positive as possible. Is there anything in the areas of Endostatin, bone-marrow transplants or any exotic cocktail that we can consider?"*

Our reaching out for help never ceased. Because her level of pain kept increasing, the doctor had Nancy stop the patches and start stronger and longer-lasting pain medication. This helped but did not override all the pain.

It came to a head on the following Sunday. The two of us were out on the deck having coffee. It was a beautiful morning but one we could not enjoy. Virtually from the outset Nancy complained about the rather sharp pain at the base of her frontal rib cage. A call to the doctor sent us right back to the hospital. A call to Nancy's mother arranged care for the boys.

The poor guys; their faces manifested their bewilderment. Actually, that's how we felt, too. This time the pain was coming from a difference source. We could only tell them—again!—that their mother had to see the doctor. I felt so deeply sorry for them. I know my eyes were burning from the tears. I hugged them hard. Once again, there was no response from them; just two quiet boys.

Returning to the hospital brought with it the hope that her pain would be relieved. As to the high probability of more bad news, we wouldn't be disappointed.

Most people can point to a period in their life that can be described as the absolute worst. The upcoming period was ours.

CHAPTER 9

NANCY IS TAKEN FROM US

In the hospital, Nancy was hooked up to a morphine drip machine. She was hurting. It was difficult to know what was going into her body, given the numerous tubes and wires connected to her. Her pain level slowly decreased. She slept a good part of the afternoon and evening.

The doctor was in the room early the next morning. Interestingly, very little had been or was being done relative to tests. The doctor did listen to Nancy's heart and lungs and inquired about the level and source of pain. The doctor then asked Nancy's sister and me to join her in another room.

We followed her to a small, empty visitor's room. It's difficult to pinpoint what it was, but we knew something was in the air; something was different about the doctor's demeanor. She was her usual calm, pleasant self, but an intangible change had taken place.

I can remember my fear as we went into that room. The kindly, gentle doctor described the state of affairs. The end had come for Nancy. The cancer now had spread through much of her body and most particularly, it had attacked her liver aggressively. The disturbing fear that had been partially hidden in my subconscious now rushed to the foreground. I started to shake.

Nancy's sister, meanwhile, appeared to listen and absorb the details. The words conveyed to us were absolutely heartbreaking. My God, that was so difficult to hear. What a sinking feeling. It left me virtually without energy. The doctor's compassionate demeanor did little to change the numbness I felt.

The doctor then recommended that Nancy stay in the hospital where she could be kept comfortable. In a day or two they would move her to another floor where, in essence, she would await death. Her sister and I were both in tears.

The dreaded expectations that had hovered overhead were now before our eyes. It was surreal. This could not be happening. This woman was only forty-six years old. She was the mother of two young boys. Why her? No, something was terribly wrong here. Why not me? There had to be a mistake. The range of profound emotions that paraded through my mind and heart seemed endless.

My experience in matters dealing with death was very limited. Three years earlier my mother had died; however, it was a very different situation. She had been in a full-care facility and, a month earlier, had celebrated her 100th birthday. I tried to visit her daily during the several years she spent at that facility. Her physical abilities had been on the decline for two or three years as the result of a series of small strokes which left her unable to talk.

One afternoon as I was leaving, she took my hand and squeezed it harder and held it longer than she normally did. Later, I wondered if there were a signal in that grip.

Later that evening I received a phone call from one of the nurses informing me that my mother had just passed. Regardless of her age and physical condition the suddenness of her death was a terrific blow.

I cried a lot on the way to her bedside. I'll never forget standing at the side of her bed looking at someone who had given me life and who had been such a strong and prominent part of it. What hit me, too, was the realization that this integral part of the family root system was gone. Inasmuch as my father had died when I was fifteen, my sister and I were the remaining "hierarchy" on both sides of our families' lineage in the United States.

Beginning that Sunday night, Nancy's sister, a daughter-in-law or a dear friend who happened to be a nurse would spend the entire night in Nancy's room. A cot was put in the room for these guardian angels and they ministered to Nancy as best they could.

During the next day or so the signs of deterioration became more obvious despite the morphine machine that kept Nancy reasonably pain-free. This led her to doze off frequently. Without fail the dosage I noted as I left in the afternoon was always higher the next morning.

It was difficult being at home with the boys. They were frightened, as was I. Once I explained the situation in fairly direct terms, they dealt with the matter either by staying in their rooms during the time they were home, or by visiting their grandparent. At home they quite often sought me out just to hug, with no words needed. They knew their mother was dying. We just didn't know when.

I wanted to cry most of the time. Natural as this was, I didn't want to add more gloom to the already dreary atmosphere. Members of the family frequently checked on us and tried to lighten up our morale.

I was on a conveyor belt shuttling between the hospital and home. Fortunately, the boys were in school so I could be at Nancy's side as much as possible during the day. It was so difficult to share her deteriorating condition with our sons, particularly without tears being shed. I had taken them to see her on a Sunday night and again two days later. The Tuesday visit was traumatic. By this time Nancy was floating between sleep (or was it unconsciousness?) and being quasi-alert. Fortunately, she was fully aware of her boys' presence. She smiled broadly. They both wore their R.O.T.C uniforms, a touch that really pleased her. Otherwise, the entire visit was so, so awkward. Conversation was disjointed and stilted. What could be said? Of course, Nancy asked how the boys were doing in school. Bless her sister, she did the best she could to inject levity. Little did we know that this would be the last time the two boys would see their mother alive.

During the early part of the week, family members and friends visited. An awareness of the finality of her condition was making its way through the ranks. No one stayed for any length of time due to Nancy's now-typical state of semi-consciousness. Except for an occasional word or brief comment, conversation was virtually non-existent.

By Wednesday simply forming words, let alone conversing, was so difficult for her. At one point her sister and I, one of us on each side of the bed, attempted to shift Nancy's position. As we made the initial effort, she all but shouted, "Stop!" This was the last word she would ever speak.

A call from her sister the morning of Thursday, March 28, 2002, had me moving as fast as possible: first to put in a call to Nancy's mother for help in getting the boys off to school, followed by making a mad dash to the hospital. I could feel it in the air, that aura, the sense of doom. Her sister's somber greeting fit the atmosphere.

Initially, I didn't know if Nancy were sleeping or unconscious. It didn't matter. Her breathing was labored and slow. Her sister asked her husband to bring her mother to the hospital as quickly as possible.

I was frightened and saturated with uncertainties. This was a first. What do you do, wait for the last breath? Or do you get the doctor in to administer the newest miracle drug? You don't just stand there and wait for someone to die, especially your wife, the mother of your children. Perhaps I was experiencing a degree of panic rather than uncertainty.

Her sister, on the other hand, seemed to be handling the situation much better. She held a damp, cool towel to Nancy's forehead and spoke words of assurance to her. She was walking Nancy through her final moments by whispering encouragements like, "It's okay to let go."

I did not want her to let go. I did not want to let go of her. Her breathing became labored, heavy and uneven. Then it came—the final breath. It was a deep inhale then everything stopped. There was no discernible exhale. It seemed as though we were in a state of suspended animation.

Impulsively, I wanted to get a doctor or nurse into that room ASAP. There had to be a way of getting Nancy back. We just couldn't let her go. Shortly, the nurse arrived. She placed her stethoscope at several points across Nancy's chest. Then, shaking her head, she quietly confirmed, "She's gone."

Nancy's mother and her sister's husband arrived shortly after the nurse left. One of my sons from my previous marriage also came. Needless to say, there was much crying and hugging. How very difficult for a mother to see her daughter lying there lifeless. And to have lost her at such a young age.

During this outpouring of grief, Nancy's doctor arrived. She listened for any sign of life. There was none. It was final; Nancy was gone. The doctor lingered for a few minutes offering what sympathy she could. What could she say to make a difference? Nonetheless, she tried. She is a sweet, compassionate woman.

I don't remember how much time passed before the others left. Finally, I was alone in the room. In a numb state I sat in a chair near the bed. All the stops opened; nothing could stem the flood of tears and the sobbing. Slowly the outpouring subsided. My breathing was more of a panting, interrupted by an occasional double inhale. I just stared ahead at nothing; I wasn't capable of forming thoughts. My emotional center had been demolished.

My stare slowly shifted to Nancy. If there were a modicum of any positive outcome in the room it was the hint of peacefulness about her. Yes, all the pain was gone. The torture of the past nine months existed no longer. The transition was from that day-to-day, treatment-to-treatment, endless agony Nancy experienced, coupled with fear, to the now; the now that would be forever and in that forever I would no longer be blessed with the beauty of Nancy in my life.

Bewilderment set in. Even in a state of mental fogginess, my mind wrestled with what all this could mean. Why had the fickle finger of fate turned in this direction? *Why her? Why wasn't I the one taken?* There I was at seventy-four. *Why not me?* What sense did taking Nancy make, a young woman at age forty-six with two young children? *Why her? Why not me? Why? Why? Why?*

There was no answer. Only God knew. At some point I thought I could understand why God would want this beautiful person with Him in heaven. At the same time, however, it made more sense to leave Nancy here on earth as long as possible to add her beautiful gifts to the world.

I'm not sure how long I sat there looking at Nancy. I was in some other space. I didn't want to leave her. That would have made it completely final. Eventually, the thought of our sons entered my mind. They had to be told. I rose and stood by the bed. I bent over and kissed her forehead and whispered that I would make her proud of our sons. That ushered in more sobbing.

Yes, the boys were next. They were in school and I had to let them know. A task no one would want. Somehow, I had to regain my composure before seeing them. I had to be strong for their sakes. Why did it have to be this way? How cruel.

CHAPTER 10

LETTING THE BOYS KNOW

I joined the others in the waiting room. By now the mood was more conversational, although one look at their eyes evidenced their recent crying. Any conversation was short-lived due to the unfortunate necessity of sharing the horrible news with the boys. Thankfully, one of my older sons insisted on accompanying me. As we were leaving, Nancy's parents decided to host a gathering of family and friends at their house. We'd all need that.

We went to Scott's school first. Telling him he'd lost his mother would be heart-wrenching even though he was aware that the end was near. He had been so close to her. We had found it easy to be close to Scott throughout his early years. He was a fun and cuddly guy, so friendly and outgoing. Nancy had been especially attentive to him. She read to him at bedtime virtually every evening and cuddled with him as part of their morning ritual.

Perhaps the closeness was, in part, the result of problems Scott experienced during the early stage of life. At a very early point it was clear that there were problems within his intestinal tract. He didn't have bowel movements for days, his stomach becoming very bloated. The results of rectal biopsies, which were extremely painful, led to medication that finally resolved the problem. Traumatic experiences like that, particularly at such an early age, easily could lead a mother to form an especially strong bond with her child.

Who could fathom the degree to which Scott's thirteen-year-old mind and heart would grasp the significance of what had happened to his mother over the preceding long months? And who could understand the impact on this young boy when told that he no longer had a mother? I've pondered the point of which situation would have the greatest impact on a young person; the sudden death of a loved one or one that, in our case, spanned a nine-month period. Without question, the former would carry with it great shock. The bewilderment we frequently noticed on our boys' faces, as well as in their behavior, signaled very little regarding the depth of their understanding of the reality of what was happening to their mother. It's tragic in any and all cases.

As we approached Scott's school, it was difficult to keep from crying. Fortunately, my son was driving and was able to maintain a calm front. The minute we walked into the office, the reason for our being there was clear. I'm sure my puffy red eyes precluded the need for words. After the receptionist called Scott's classroom, we went outside to wait. Within minutes, Scott came out accompanied by two teachers, both "angels". After seeing us, especially my reddened face, his head turned down and his eyes were fixed on the dull-gray concrete. He came to me and we clenched each other hard. I could hear the teachers attempting to stifle their sobs. Oh, Lord, it was so difficult.

My older son, though slightly red-eyed, had maintained his composure. As we walked to the car he offered Scott wonderful, comforting words of encouragement. As we drove away, Scott looked out the window and remained quiet. It was his turn to attempt to digest and process what had happened and what it meant.

Instead of picking up Ed right away, we drove directly to Nancy's parents' house. I wanted Scott to be with family; with people he knew. I also felt it would be too emotional at that point if both boys were together in the car. By the time we arrived at the house, several members of the extended families were there along with some of our close friends.

Now it was Ed's turn.

I decided to go to Ed's school by myself and I'm not sure why. I would most likely cry the minute I saw him. Whereas I had sensed a more emotional encounter with Scott and had accepted my son's offer to accompany me to his school, I felt strong enough to find and tell Ed the news on my own.

In the attendance office at his high school, I asked if Ed could be excused for the rest of the day. When asked why, I said his mother had just passed away. The woman wrote something on a slip of paper and had a student deliver it to Ed's room.

I waited for him at the edge of the school's quad. Within minutes he appeared. I studied his face as we walked toward each other. He displayed no discernible emotion. When he was a few yards from me, I started shaking my head slowly. We embraced even before I finished telling him what had transpired. The tears coursed down my cheeks in silent sorrow. Ed was still. The people around us must have wondered what had happened. We separated. His eyes were red. He seemed very much in control of his emotions, which was so like him. Throughout his life, and particularly during his long bout with cancer, he had not been prone to expressing what he felt. Yes, he cried and moaned at having needles inserted or in reaction to the debilitating nausea that accompanied chemotherapy, but otherwise, he didn't let on.

With my arm around his shoulders, we headed for the car. He was very quiet and remained so for most of the short drive to his grandparents' home. I related, as gently as possible, his mother's final hours. I felt so sorry for him. How can a person comprehend the way a young mind processes such tragic events? Perhaps the adult mind assumes its interpretation of reactive feelings is universal. Perhaps we exaggerate how the young receptors will translate the impact of events like the loss of a mother. I guess we'll never know.

By the time Ed and I reached the wake, the gathering numbered something on the order of thirty. The noise level was high, which was good. Crying was at a minimum. Also good. It was mid-afternoon and people were indulging in alcoholic beverages, which led to laughter; certainly that was good. The mood from earlier had evaporated. Ed and Scott seemed to join in the spirit of the moment.

Nancy's family and friends continued to serve food, so the event ran well into the evening. In the back of my mind, however, loomed the inevitable, the boys and I would have to go home. How I dreaded that. I even gave some thought to going to a motel just to avoid what I knew awaited us, a silent house full of raw memories of Nancy—and there would no Nancy. Fortunately, two of my older children offered to spend the night with us, which helped tremendously.

It was quite late when we arrived home and the boys looked like they were ready for bed. Late or not, they wouldn't be going to school the next day. I anticipated a rough day for all of us. As they were heading for their rooms, I decided to get together with them to talk, and if possible, to see if we could ease out of this horrible day. But what would I say? I didn't have a script. Maybe it would be best to let them share their thoughts or feelings, if they felt like it.

We remained silent for many seconds as we sat on Ed's bed. Once it became apparent that they weren't in a sharing mood, I decided to say a few words. In a subdued voice, I touched lightly on the point that their mother was no longer suffering and, best of all, she was in heaven with God and how happy God must be to have such a beautiful person with Him. I added that there was a good chance that my mother had been there to greet her. I mentioned, too, that we'd have to be strong for each other and to support each other. We said a few prayers together. Before separating we had a solid group hug.

I was too emotionally drained to know if I were sleepy or not. However, I was alert enough to realize how frightened and insecure I felt over facing the real world that awaited all of us. Oh, how I dreaded the next day. How would I handle tomorrow and the tomorrows beyond?

The first tomorrow was virtually packed with necessary responsibilities before it even opened. Plans had to be made for a religious service and Nancy's burial. At the time I had made arrangements for my mother burial four years earlier, I had purchased burial plots for Nancy and me as well. Beyond that, there was no apparent need to set in place future plans for the two of us.

Fortunately, former neighbors owned a mortuary, such relieving me of the need to spend time on the telephone making these important arrangements. Also, I had the elements of my mother's burial to fall back on. Importantly, I had kept in touch with the kindly priest who had presided over a religious service for my mother in the cemetery's chapel and, as well, at the grave site. The fact that he had married Nancy and me swerved as a very meaningful connection. His comments about Nancy were so warm and appropriate for the families and close friends in attendance. I felt throughout that Nancy would have been very pleased with the caring manner in which the procedures were carried out.

It was difficult during the services to maintain a constant focus. On the one hand, I was struggling with my emotions and, without question, they were deep. More than once I posed the oft-repeated question to myself, *Oh Lord, Why her? Why not me?* Of course, I was deeply concerned about the boys' emotional condition. Even though they were sitting next to me it was difficult to gauge how they were doing inside.

Their eyes were reddened, otherwise it appeared as though they were doing ok. The presence of family members and close friends appeared to bolster their emotional strength.

A very special tableau was created by six of my children, including Ed and Scott, carrying Nancy's casket the short distance to the grave site.

Following the burial services, we once again repaired to Nancy's parent's home to bring closure to this extremely sad occasion.

Following the burial services, we once again repaired to Nancy's parent's home to bring closure to this extremely sad occasion.

The next event to plan was a memorial. Nancy's sister I coordinated our efforts to find a suitable venue to accommodate the many invitees we expected to attend. Well over 100 guests were there, including many of the staff and "angels" from the Charter School. Certain of the staff offered wonderful memories of the gracious and caring mother that, to them, characterized Nancy. Others also gave heart-warming comments. Many a tear were shed. It was a wonderful testimonial to Nancy's popularity and to the great respect she deserved.

Well, we had accomplished the first of the tomorrows to come. It was a deeply sad first, but our good bye to our beloved Nancy was done with great care and with the dignity that she deserved. She would forever be in our hearts and in the boys' and my home. Now it was time to prepare for the next tomorrow and all that would follow.

CHAPTER 11

CONFRONTED BY THE REAL WORLD

The surreal world in which we had lived for weeks started to dissipate shortly after the memorial. The numbness began wearing off, although often enough I still found myself slumped in a chair staring into space. At these times, there seemed to be little or no brain activity. Slowly, the magnitude and intricacies of what lay ahead for the three of us became exaggerated in my mind. It seemed as though some invisible force was pulling down my brow, giving me heavy eyes and leaving me with a horrible sinking feeling.

I hated this sense of helplessness and futility. The slump seemed deeper and more incisive than any from thirty years earlier. Although I'd always considered myself an up-beat person, the weight that pressed down on my entire being at times was overwhelming. From time to time, self-pity would visit me. The rawness of the real world started to kick in. I'm sure that the good Lord became tired of my never-ending petitioning to have Nancy returned to us.

Nights were difficult early on. Because I'd been sleeping on the couch, it was awkward to once again sleep in our bed. What a strange feeling to be in that bed by myself. I remember waking up during the night fearful that I might have disturbed Nancy by moving too much or too abruptly. More than once I was tempted to head for the couch. And, more than once, sleep was preceded by crying. Crying? Sobbing would be more accurate. Oh, how many times I sobbed during the early days. It could hit me while showering or preparing a meal or while driving. What loneliness and misery. It was incredible. It hurt so much.

Presumably, I was reacting to a combination of things. Nancy's presence in the house was powerful. I expected to see her every time I turned around. I expected her to come through a door at any moment. And, in the evening, my mind told me she'd be home from teaching at any moment. I'd come home from my office looking forward to our comfortable tête-à-têtes on the deck. Her voice and her laugh were in the air. Oh, how I missed her.

I couldn't grasp the idea that I was now in charge of everything. All decisions would be mine for some time to come. I just didn't know how I could handle even the predictable future. And, without question, the well-being of the boys was paramount.

The trauma associated with my having been left to raise my five children 30 years earlier surfaced often enough. For the post part, that other life could seem so distant and foreign, yet it increasingly occupied center stage in my mind. How had I coped in that other life? How was I going to handle my new life? Without question, raising five children on my own was a monumental endeavor; however, there was no way of realistically comparing the loss of a wife to divorce with the tragic death of a wife.

As in the past, it seemed like the end of the world for me. My despair often was profound. I was so ill prepared to manage a household – at least, that's how my mind exaggerated the matter. Nevertheless, I wanted daily life to stay as normal as possible for Ed and Scott. This task seemingly bordered on the impossible, at least in the near term. While attempting to cope with the growing realities of daily life, my mind constantly replayed the unsolvable mystery of Nancy's dying first. All of our planning and reasoning, though never discussed directly, had been based on sound logic — I would be the first to go. Why her?, why not me? replayed itself in my mind over and over.

Ten or twelve years earlier, we'd had a revocable trust drawn up so that Nancy and the children would be cared for in the event of my death. Following the birth of each son I initiated investments so that funds for college or other needs would be available to ease any financial burden for Nancy once I expired. Who would have bet against my being the first to leave this world? Her early death made no sense at all. Again, why her?, why not me?.

Although it was difficult for the boys to focus on their homework, it was fortunate, as on several recent occasions, that they were in school. The teachers were understanding and helpful. It was so good for the boys to be around their friends and to stay occupied. And it was good for me to have to busy myself by getting them ready for school, preparing their lunches, and seeing them off on the bus. That accomplished, I was now free to go to my office. Frequently, though, I would bring work home so that I could mix necessary house work with professional work. Focusing on professional work was convenient only while they were in school.

Nancy and I had developed our individual assignments. For the most part she attended to matters in the house such as cooking, shopping, and overseeing the basic needs of the boys. She did the cooking and I did the cleaning. My responsibilities chiefly were to maintain our half-acre river-front property. In other words, the inside was Nancy's territory and the outside was mine — with one huge exception. Nancy loved gardening and she had spent as much time as possible in her garden. What would happen to her garden? She had been so good at it. Me? I knew so very little about gardening. As with so many other categories, I expected to be on the learning curve for a long time.

Nancy's teaching hours usually had been scheduled during the late afternoon and early evening. Appreciating the fact that I had a business to run, she'd always prepared a warm-up dinner for the boys and me on the evenings she taught. This, of course, had become increasingly difficult the weeks preceding her death. Once again, thanks to the guardian angels for their help.

From the outset, preparing meals and the related shopping were challenges. How had I done this as head of my previous household? I remembered trying to scope out a week's worth of meals prior to venturing into the shopping arena. As for cooking skills, any I had developed in my other life basically had vanished. Also, as in the past, preparing dinners was the most challenging. And, once again, I tried to ignore the lure of fast foods. Sadly, I could not look forward to my mother's periodic visits and her help in the cooking and sewing departments.

Fortunately, our current house is relatively small and compact. And we have a cleaning lady. Dividing up chores between the boys was much simpler although the range and nature of their complaints closely resembled those of the older generation.

Laundry – that was another annoying issue. Initially, I had to re-learn how to use a washing machine and all that goes with selecting temperatures, colors and material. It took me awhile to regain developing a pattern or schedule. Still, I much prefer laundry to cooking.

Often enough during the early stages of this new life, I felt my age. Emotions, pressures and anxieties surely contributed. At the end of any given day, regardless of what had transpired, I was a tired soul. I may have felt my age, but at the same time I didn't go around advertising it. Yes, I think I wanted people to be impressed with my situation, but just to a point. I wasn't going to let the numbers game get in my way.

Thank the Lord I had my religion to sustain me, although I'm sure that God got a little tired of hearing both my complaints and my petitions.

Also during the early stage of our new life, I was very conscious of how the boys were handling their emotions. They were hard to read. They were quiet most of the time and kept to themselves more than before. Logically, they had to be missing Nancy's beautiful energy and vivaciousness that filled the house.

One episode that hit me particularly hard involved a diary my cousin had given to Scott at the memorial. At the front of the diary she'd written a note suggesting he write about his feelings whenever he felt like it. She mentioned that it would help him get through this terrible period.

I happened to see the diary on the floor next to his bed one morning shortly after he'd left for school. I wanted to see if he'd written in it. I felt guilty about invading his privacy, but I needed to know how he was doing emotionally… if, indeed, he'd written in the diary.

I was sorry I had opened it. He had written:

> *"I'm actually not sure who to write this to. I'm not sure what to write. This is my first entry. Dear mom, I think dad has been the loneliest in the house. I'm glad I have friends to talk to. I think about you a lot. Every time I think about you I want to cry. During the time you have passed away dad has had to do all the things you did. When dad told me you only had a couple of days to live, I started to cry. He told me we would have to come together as a family to get through this. I think I cried the hardest when I heard the news about you. The last time I saw you was the night before you died. I love you, mom. I have to go. I'm crying."*

I can't remember crying harder. I'm not sure how long I sat on his bed, with my head in my hands. I was so impressed with his concern for me. His comments were so full of innocence. I felt so deeply for my thirteen-year-old boy.

A more or less positive event arrived shortly after Nancy died – Easter vacation. One of my older sons arranged for the three of us to spend the week with him at his home on the island of Maui. That was a Godsend. The week was a terrific distraction for Ed and Scott. My son outfitted them with boogie-boards and snorkeling equipment and away they went.

Me? I had the luxury of doing whatever I wanted. Usually that amounted to doing nothing but letting my brain wander, trying to read and dozing. It was a timely blessing.

The Hawaiian outing reminded me of years earlier when I hadn't had children from a previous marriage to look to for this type of help. After my first wife left I had felt the need to keep my five children occupied whenever possible and this often took the form of trips. On one occasion I rented an RV and we visited Yosemite Valley. For another outing we rented a houseboat and plied the rivers and sloughs of Northern California's Delta region.

In both cases I succumbed to cabin fever. Being cooped up with five children was not a relaxing proposition. Noble as my intentions had been, it really got to me. For one thing, I was in need of adult companionship. Being alone with children any length of time could be really stressful. Without question, there were many pleasurable moments, thanks in large measure to the wonderful natural environments we visited.

Returning to the real world from Hawaii was difficult, indeed. However, school once again was a plus for the three of us. I made every effort to develop a schedule and discipline. I had to pay more attention to my business. Bringing work home was okay to a point but I often needed information from the files in my office. It was not a good arrangement. Further, it was much easier to concentrate on the detective work needed to uncover Mother Nature's hidden stores of oil and gas at the office than in my home. Unfortunately, there wasn't enough space in our house to accommodate sufficient working space for me let alone space for my many file cabinets. I'd just have to struggle along.

At home it was too easy to have my professional thinking overridden by domestic matters such as what we would have for dinner, whether I had transferred the laundry to the drier, and the like. Of course, when the boys were home the level of distractions rose. So much of this was reminiscent of earlier years. Needless to say, there was a huge difference between the noise level generated by five children versus that of two. At seventy-four, my supply of patience was was being drained.

In time, the lifestyle began to have a telling effect on my work. More than once I was tempted to close my office and, in one way or another, set up a workplace at home. And more than once, the suggestion that I retire was put in front of me by my older children. Yes, it made sense to retire; however, I was engaged in a business that held my fascination and, of course, I couldn't ignore my obligations to my clients.

Besides, there was the matter of income. I wasn't sure if I were solvent enough to take that huge step.

Unfortunately, the fact that homework wasn't the boys' favorite activity meant I had to monitor them closely. Ed's primary strength and drives were in the Air Force Jr. R.O.T.C. program and in playing the alto clarinet in the school band.

Meanwhile, Scott's chief focus was on athletic endeavors both at school and the soccer field on Saturdays. He was blessed with exceptional athletic abilities. And, yes, there was the occasional homework.

For quite some time they had enjoyed playing one-on-one basketball in our driveway. It seemed as though the frequency had dropped during those horrible weeks just prior to Nancy's death. Now, weeks later, they were back at it. It was gratifying to watch them playing and arguing again. That was so good for them.

Neither had cared much for reading. Nancy had been so good at sitting or lying down with them and reading to them, especially with Scott. That would be a challenge for me. There was no way I could treat the boys the way she had.

In particular, she loved cuddling with Scott. Every school morning Nancy would wake up early, head for Scott's bed, then fall back asleep cuddling him. I tried to emulate this but it just didn't work. I'd get restless after a few minutes or he would not so subtly let me know that my efforts weren't working.

Suffice to say that I was trying to keep their lives as normal as possible.

We were faced with one of the difficult emotional hurdles shortly after our return from Hawaii – Mother's Day. I had expected it to be rough on all of us, and it was.

Nancy's mother and the boys and I, flowers in hand, visited Nancy's grave.

Barely two months had gone by since her death. Things were still so fresh in our hearts and minds. Very little was said; quiet prevailed. Each of us dealing with the hurt in his or her own way.

The well-groomed cemetery resembled a flower garden, which added to the beauty of day. The cloudless, deep-blue sky and the mild temperature seemed to have been programmed for this very special day. We certainly weren't alone; many visitors were there either standing silently or arranging flowers at a grave site.

It was easy for me to feel sorry for myself during this early period. Self-pity or not, though, there was a job to be done. Any concerns for my well-being had to take a back seat to the needs and welfare of Ed and Scott. The task would be very difficult and demanding. More than once I asked myself if I could handle it. No, age seventy-four did not bring a wealth of energy to the role of a single parent to two teenage boys. However, I was blessed ever so thankfully with good health. And I would need it. There was much more to come.

CHAPTER 12

THE TOMORROWS
START IN EARNEST

The summer following Nancy's death was a long one even though both boys attended summer school. The five-week classes made up for deficiencies during the previous academic year. More than once I reminded them that their mother would be so proud of them if they applied themselves and did well in school. The loss of their mother exacerbated their somewhat weak performances. This manifested itself more in Scott. Unfortunately, the problem would take on exponential dimensions during the coming years.

Visiting their schools for open houses or back-to-school nights during the regular semester was easy enough. As problems in the academic arena surfaced, an awkwardness evolved. Perhaps it had been there the whole time. At any rate, I became increasingly conscious of it after Nancy's death. As my treks to see teachers and principals grew in frequency, so did the realization that a seventy-five-year-old, gray-haired man presenting himself as a teenager's father was anything but the norm. Initially, I could sense the teachers and students wondering what Scott's grandfather was doing at school. The matter had recycled in my mind more than once in the past; however, it hadn't been a strong focal point, but now I was becoming more and more aware of it. I certainly didn't want to be an embarrassment to my children. Well, here was another item to add to the growing list of adjustments I'd have to make. I wasn't sure, though, just what the adjustments would be.

The five-week summer sessions squelched any plans for significant travel. I would have loved to have had a break; to have taken a vacation. I did manage a couple of times to get away for a day to have lunch with my fraternity brothers in Newport Beach. Otherwise a mix of family members and friends catered to our social needs by involving the boys in various activities. Thank the Lord we weren't alone despite the void in our home and lives. Keeping busy was the first order of business.

Just prior to the close of the regular school year, I arranged for Ed to learn to drive. He was a month short of turning seventeen. We'd failed to initiate lessons following his sixteenth birthday because of the incredible sequence of tragic medical events. Nevertheless, he obtained his driver's permit just after his July 4th birthday. I was hopeful that, once he became a full-fledged driver, he'd be able to help me with errands.

I was more than ready for the schools to start up by the time the summer of 2002 ended. Ed would be a Junior; Scott an eighth-grader. I'm not so sure I would have felt the same about their return to school had I been able to crystal-ball the future. More scholastic and medical problems awaited us. I knew better than to ask, "What's next?"

The schools opened in August. I was happy to have more time to myself. During the summer it had become clear that my patience was growing shorter. I could sense a transition. Whereas I had become so protective of the boys, particularly of their emotional well being, I found myself barking more, arguing with Ed more, and just plain airing my irritations more frequently.

Discussions with Ed commonly digressed into snotty arguments. More than once Nancy had cautioned me to choose my confrontations with him carefully. The two of us could argue about anything or everything! Neither of us wanted to give up or allow a point to be made by the other.

Scott had been cut from different fabric. His was a calmer nature. Certainly he could be obstinate; however, he wasn't one to look for an argument. He avoided them. Nancy had been so good at reading both boys' characters.

Their schooling, of course, allowed me more office time as well as more flexibility to program my brain for the new rigors of family life.

Often during my runs to the office I stopped in at the small chapel at a nearby church. I would just sit with my eyes closed and let my mind go in whatever direction it chose. These breaks were very rehabilitating. Naturally, I prayed a lot. I asked for help and guidance. Perhaps I was hoping for a magic dust to cover our lives and make everything okay.

No sooner had school started than another emotional event confronted us – Nancy's birthday. She would have been forty-seven. Interestingly, Ed was the one to give the heads-up for that occasion. As things evolved, he became very reliable at reminding the family of approaching dates, particularly where his mother was concerned. The occasion was acknowledged when we and Nancy's mother took flowers to the gravesite, this later followed by a family dinner.

Even more emotions poured out a few days after Nancy's birthday. I happened to notice Scott's diary on the desk in his bedroom. It had been several months since I had read his first entry, that deeply emotional entry. Once again I was curious to know if additional entries had been made. The "guilt angel" showed up on my shoulder; nevertheless, I wanted to know how he was doing.

A new entry had been written a few days before Nancy's birthday.

> *"Sorry it took me so long to write again. We put your leaf on the tree at the hospital today. I started school Wednesday. Dad still has to do all the work around the house. Next Friday is your birthday. We are going out to*

dinner for your birthday. I still remember the day you died. I was in 5th[h] period (Language Arts). I got called to the office. I thought it was because I had a doctor's appointment. Dad was there and he hugged me and told me that you had past away. I started to cry and so did he. We went to grandma's house. We went to the movies the other night. We came home and I thought that you would be here. But you weren't. I kept thinking that you would be here. Love you mom. 8/24/02."

Well, it had been a while since I'd had a good cry. Once again, I was so touched with the way Scott expressed himself. It was so moving that he was writing directly to his mother.

As the weeks and months progressed, so did my visits to Scott's Charter School. It would be his last year there – if he could make it through. By December, the academic problems were mounting. I don't remember how many times I went to his school to meet either with his teachers or his adviser. The guardian angels had started to shed their feathers.

Matters became very, very serious. After giving Scott every benefit of the doubt, I was informed that he would have to leave the school. Even though I'd received ample warning, it was a huge blow. There were no more rules to bend or break; they had gone through the entire book. Of course, they had to be fair to the other students. I blamed myself for having failed him. And, there we were in the middle of the school year just before the start of Christmas vacation. Merry Christmas!

There were not a lot of options. We could have tried home schooling or tutoring, but I felt that it just wouldn't work. Also, it would have tied my hands professionally. The only viable option was a nearby middle school, the one he'd attended during the summer session. We assumed this would be an automatic, perfunctory transfer. Not so!

I was somewhat surprised at the strong resistance I received from the principal. One of his first comments, and in rather terse terms, was that he wasn't inclined to accept "rejects" from the Charter School. He wasn't running a school for problem students, academic or otherwise. It took some pleading and emotional blackmailing to get him to allow Scott to attend. Honest tears came to my eyes when I described what we'd been through with his mother and the effect it was having on Scott.

It wasn't just a matter of the principal saying yea or nay; strings were attached. He drew up a contract that both Scott and I had to sign. Scott would have to maintain a "C" or better grade-point average and would have to behave like a model student. I had no problem with the last point. Thankfully Scott had always been very a very respectful person. Any complaints about his behavior had been minimal. Maintaining passing grades, on the other hand…well, that would take some doing.

Even though he'd failed at the Charter School, Scott's acceptance at the middle school improved the portents for a relatively cheerful holiday season. We were heading to the Chicago area to enjoy Christmas with my sister and brother-in-law. Always pleasurable, the addition of snow made for a more traditional Christmas and, of course, the boys loved it. For me, happy-hour with my brother-in-law did, indeed, make Christmas a very merry one.

Immediately after Christmas we joined my daughter and her husband in Milwaukee, and members of his family, to visit their upper-state cabin for a few days. Again, a great outing. Ice-skating and fishing on a frozen lake were new and novel activities for the boys. We were in a different, worry-free world. Schooling wasn't on the radar screen. Not having to make decisions, being in the company of fun-loving family members, and enjoying plentiful happy hours made for solid, healing medication. Best of all, I didn't have to prepare meals. Yes, it was a great Christmas.

The end of the year brought with it a tremendous surge of emotion.

Just look at what we'd been through. The ugliness of cancer coupled with the loss of a mother and wife can only be described as devastating. Adapting to a new lifestyle in which my age played an integral role was a raw experience, one with no guidebook.

Reflecting on the previous New Year brought tears. Remembering our hopes for traveling to Lourdes in search for a miracle was fodder for deep sadness. The inevitable search for answers, especially the attempt to understand why the fickle finger of fate had pointed in our direction, led to more head-shaking. We'd been through hell and could only hope that 2003 would bring some level of calm and stability.

Over time, I tried to condition myself to not look too far into the future and to keep my expectations low. In a sense, though, this ran counter to my penchant to anticipate as much as possible. I had a penchant for trying to minimize surprises, particularly the negative ones.

Also, I was learning that, with age, people become increasingly conservative. Maybe it was about becoming a creature of habit and avoiding change, especially upheavals. Well, those might have been valid traits; however, I had no voice in what the future held. It was too easy to expect more bad news. I wasn't disappointed.

CHAPTER 13

TRIP TO EUROPE
ON-GOING PROBLEMS AT SCHOOL

Late in 2002, my daughter came up with a tantalizing proposal — a trip to Europe during the following summer. I had taken her and her twin brother to Europe in 1977 when they were in their mid-teens to meet members of my mother's and father's families in France and England. She had loved the experience. Since her husband had never been to Europe, the idea of introducing him to the continent was intriguing. I was excited at the thought; it would be tonic for the boys and me. I experienced a strange sensation when the thought of going without Nancy came to mind. We had so enjoyed our many trips to Europe.

As the weeks and months progressed, the balancing act between keeping a close eye on the boys, trying to run my consulting practice, and planning a trip helped keep my mind off the sad side of our lives. My circle of professional associates also helped balance my life. Several days a week, a group of us teamed up for coffee or lunch to discuss the natural gas exploration business in the Sacramento Valley, to tell antiquated jokes, or just to chat. The gatherings were essential for me.

It didn't take long once school was back in session for the calls and or emails to start arriving regarding problems for both boys. Very thankfully, behavior was never an issue; it was always class work, or the lack thereof. One thing both Ed and Scott were deft at was conning me into believing neither had homework. Another favorite trick was claiming that assignments weren't due until the following week. More than once I had to contact a teacher to ferret out what was going on. Of course, the boys didn't care for that. I took this education matter very personally – I was doing a horrible job in the education arena.

All too often it was a case of taking the horse to water only to have the water ignored. I worked with them as best I could. Reluctantly and infrequently I would all but do an assignment for them. I tried everything, including a tongue-in-cheek offer to pay them to go to school, in an attempt to excite or energize them.

Both Nancy and I held Master's Degrees in our respective fields – math and geology. Each of my older children had been achievers in college, each of them with Bachelor degrees or higher. One had received a Doctorate in Computer Science from Yale; another a dual Bachelor's Degree from Stanford (Economics and French) as well as an MBA from MIT. The youngest of my older children, a high-school dropout, is a CPA.

Placing these accomplishments in front of Ed and Scott paid few dividends. My own lack of ambition during high school wasn't mentioned. Enjoyment had been the operative word. Oh, what I'd put my widowed mother through! I don't know how she coped. She must have had a direct line to God. So often I wished I had her skills in the praying department.

Interestingly, I would not have gone to college if my mother and sister hadn't teamed up for me. Another way of stating it might be, they "conspired" against me. Apparently, they did not trust my judgement as to my future plans once I was discharged from the Navy, and rightfully so. Arriving in Los Angeles on a Friday afternoon, after having been discharged, I was greeted at the train station by my mother and sister. Once the greetings and hugs were finished, my sister announced that I was enrolled in college. This shock was followed by the news that she had gone to the classes she had chosen for me, for the first two weeks of school. I couldn't believe it; I had arrived on a Friday afternoon and I would be in college on Monday. Decidedly, this was not what I had in mind upon being discharged from the service. My gosh, I had but a weekend to readjust to civilian life! In retrospect, it was one of the great blessings of my life. The GI Bill, of course, greatly facilitated my having achieved graduate school.

As the time since Nancy's death lengthened and the attention I devoted to all the facets of our lives increased, the thought of selling my practice came up more and more. That was a tough decision. I'd been in the oil and gas business for close to fifty years and I loved it. It's such an exciting field. It's detective work within the deep reaches of Mother Earth. Up until then I'd been able to gerrymander work between my office and home in an acceptable manner. Nevertheless, the increasing needs of the boys coupled with household obligations increasingly took me away from work.

With great difficulty I formulated a plan to sell my files. That necessitated sifting through thousands of documents and organizing them in a presentable style. The work required several months to accomplish. Fortunately, I was able to do much of it at home.

I also put together what I thought was an enticing letter to send to firms and individuals in my field. It was a good letter. Unfortunately, the response was minimal. Repeated revisions didn't stir up much interest. I had placed a rather hefty price tag on my files, files that included decades of research and information. They were valuable.

At the same time, my daughter and I were heavily involved with plans for the summer trip to Europe. As the weeks progressed, nervousness over Scott's schooling also progressed. Late in May, I was informed that he would not be graduating from middle school. What a jolt! My feelings were mixed; I felt so sorry for him and, at the same time, I was hugely upset with him. He just couldn't tune into the academic world. At the same time I was highly upset with myself for having failed him. I should have retained a tutor long ago.

I had known for weeks that he'd been flirting with the minimum grade-point average, still the news was a blow. I had thought the school would give him the benefit of the doubt. Not so. A meeting with the principal put the matter in black and white terms – Scott had not met the minimum requirements. He would have to go to summer school to graduate. And we were leaving for Europe in ten days.

Conjuring up the best words I could find I implored the principal to find a solution that would keep me from losing a considerable amount of money by canceling the trip. Although tough and determined, he finally agreed to a workable game plan.

During the trip Scott would be a keen observer. He would keep a journal, not one that merely stated what he'd done on a particular day, but one that would provide insights into what he was learning about different cultures, historical events and the like. He would then compile a significant report on the contents of his journal and his observations. Fair enough. It would make the trip that more meaningful for all of us. And, as it turned out, each of us became more astute with our own observations. I found myself noticing more details and gaining different perspectives as we visited different countries.

The trip itself was outstanding. The six of us – Ed, Scott and me, plus my daughter, my son-in-law and their twelve-year-old son (my grandson) – made a wonderful team. It was a three-week, train-based run that started in Frankfurt and included Amsterdam, Paris, Murren (Switzerland), Rome, Venice and Munich. Nancy and I had been to each of these cities but chiefly by car, but never by train.

Whether in a compartment or in an open car, we relaxed, enjoyed the scenery and boned up on our next stop. It seemed like we did a lot of laughing, too. The boys, of course, couldn't sit still too long and ended up scouting out virtually every car of each train. They really enjoyed this mode of travel. From time to time they got a little too adventuresome and had to be reined in.

We frequently, reminded Scott about his project. That was a tough one. Thinking about school matters was totally inconsistent with the pleasures and novelty of traveling. In one way or another and wherever we were, the adults came up with an observation or two for him. At first, he would jot down a note on a pad he carried in his backpack. Not surprisingly, as we moved along, the chore fell to me. This was an easy one to predict even before leaving home. During happy hour or dinner, we frequently reviewed what we had learned that day. This actually made the trip more fulfilling.

The highlight of our trip was Murren. That was my fifth time visiting this incredible piece of real estate. It was Nancy and my favorite. While there, I spent quite a bit of quiet time reflecting on the wonderful times the two of us had enjoyed during our travels in general and, particularly, at that heavenly spot.

At the same time, I remember pondering my emotional state. Nancy had passed away close to a year and a half earlier. Certainly, the pain of losing her had diminished during the intervening period. My feelings as I reflected on our visits to Murren were more nostalgic than hurtful. There was a distinct warmth associated with the memories.

Once the boys were old enough, we'd taken them there twice. We had great times trekking through this Swiss paradise. I wondered if they connected this visit with ones in the past, and especially if they remembered being there with their mother. They showed no sign of this so I left the matter alone. Suffice to say that they were having a great time. By virtue of their comments and actions, it appeared that their memories of a year and a half ago had also lessened significantly.

During the trip, Nancy's name came up more than once. Fortunately, they didn't seem to be bothered by any discussion regarding her.

The stay in Murren was highlighted by Ed's eighteenth birthday. The celebration was a good one, thanks to the appropriate libation (Champaign) and the gifts we had brought from home. Trying to envision Ed as an adult would take some doing. I couldn't imagine him voting for the president of the United States.

Typically, when in a city or town, we'd move around in a tight group. However, as the trip progressed annoyances occasionally cropped up; these usually because of something one of the boys had done or said. More than once this resulted in some yelling. Accordingly, we found it beneficial from time to time to break up into smaller groups. It was good for all of us.

There were sobering moments, too. Each of us, particularly the boys, was very impressed with the Anne Frank museum in Amsterdam. The manner in which her tragic story is perpetuated fit right in with Scott's project. Also, her youth was something the boys could relate to.

The beaches at Normandy and the related history also were of great interest. Even though my daughter and I had been there before, it still fascinated us. I was impressed with how the boys virtually automatically showed their respect while at the American military cemetery at Omaha Beach. There was no playing around or loud talking.

An enjoyable adjunct to our stay in Paris was having dinner with two of my first cousins and other members of the family. My cousin's father and my mother were brother and sister, both of them born and raised in the Basque country of southern France. Of particular note was their father's (my uncle's) exploits during World War II. He had been a career officer in the French Army and was one of the last to be evacuated from Dunkirk. After the fall of France, he returned to civilian life and worked with the Resistance in Paris – that is, until he was forced to escape from France. Because of this work with the Resistance, he was wanted by the German Gestapo. With the help of fellow members of the Resistance, he and others made their arduous escape over the Pyrenees mountains into Spain. He then made his way to Morocco where he rejoined the French forces and later became a member of General Eisenhower's staff. Because of the logistical skills he had exhibited in North Africa, he was awarded the Legion of Merit by the U.S. government, the highest military award given to a foreign member of the military. Additionally, the British Government awarded him its Order of the British Empire, its highest honor for a foreigner. The French also awarded him its highest military honors. He retired as a General.

It seemed that during each visit with members of my French family over the years, some aspect of my uncle's exploits was touched on. I can't remember anyone traveling with me not being fascinated with him. Everyone thoroughly enjoyed hearing about his achievements.

One evening our group and my cousins rendezvoused in a very charming restaurant in Paris's left-bank Latin Quarter. I had studied as a Fulbright Scholar at the nearby Sorbonne during my post-university days so I was somewhat familiar with the area. I was pleased that my travel companions, especially Ed and Scott, had the opportunity to team up with our cousins.

My cousin, Jean, took charge of all facets of ordering, and this in his excellent Parisian French. This was not a touristy restaurant so it allowed our group the opportunity to enjoy a different culinary experience. It intrigued me that ordering the various wines, a different variety with each course, took almost as long as ordering dinner.

For a change of pace for us "gringos", the superb dinner opened with an "aperitif" wine and ended with champagne or a choice of "digestif" liqueurs and a platter of delicious pastries.

Ed commented on the salad being served after the main course rather than before. Noticeable, too, were the numerous changes of plates and silverware. Poor Scott was asked numerous times if he were at least making mental notes of these differences. I think he would have preferred to just eat.

There was much laughter during the dinner. Ed and Scott laughed as much as the adults. A good part of this was the result of trying to communicate. The consumption of wine contributed to the merriment as well. Interacting with family members in a foreign country and the challenges of communication were such good experiences for the boys.

This was very much in line with my mother having been such a strong advocate of maintaining close ties with family, distance and language barriers notwithstanding. This applied to both sides of the English Channel, as my father's family resided on the Isle of Man.

The trip put the boys and me in a different world. Nancy was certainly with us but in an entirely different way. The conviviality of our fellow travelers added to the medicinal effects. Sadly, as we inched our way home, the medicine started to wear off. I was not anxious to re-enter the world of household management nor, without question, the world of education. School was scheduled to start soon after our return. What could we expect from the principal at Scott's school? Would Scott pull off his assignment and be allowed to enter high school?

Our homecoming was a quiet one. Fortunately, there had been no problems during our absence. Because schools would begin in just two weeks, it was essential that Scott plunge into his report-writing project. As things turned out he did a very credible job. It was time to get the report into the principal's hands.

Upon arriving at Scott's school we were informed that the principal had been transferred to another school. Because of school policies they could not let us know to which school he was now assigned. I was convinced that a jinx had been placed on Scott and schooling. This was not what we needed, given the very short time remaining. We were directed to the school district office only to learn the same thing – policy prevented them from telling us where the principal was located.

Since the person we needed to address at the district office was unavailable, we made two trips before we finally found the right person. After pleading Scott's case we were told that the district office would contact the principal and decide the best course of action. After an inordinate wait, we were told to leave the report at the district office. Someone would review it and communicate the results to the principal. This had developed into an unnecessarily monumental situation.

Finally and fortunately, the district contacted us to let us know that Scott could attend high school. This was excellent news, but it only went so far. Incredibly, because Scott's name was not on the list of new students arriving from Middle School, the high school couldn't enroll him. Back to the district office we went. By now we were almost on a first-name basis with the staff. A week into the new school year, Scott started attending high school. How much more of this could this body and mind of mine take?

Both boys were now at the same school. It had been one hell of an effort in Scott's case. We'd have to wait and see how things would work out.

All along I'd felt that, had Nancy been with us, Scott's problems never would have reached the point they had. Could I have done more or done things better to minimize the problems that both boys had faced at their schools? Yes, of course.

Well, much more would come before the end of the year. The remaining months were charged both with the predictable and unpredictable.

CHAPTER 14

MORE TRAVEL AND THE HOLIDAYS

The school year had barely begun when, on a September morning, a fateful phone call came. A company was interested in purchasing my files, and at a very reasonable price. This was great. Still, weeks would be required to satisfy the company's due-diligence investigation. The experience was a rigorous one. Several meetings were held before the final OK was given.

A strange sensation came over me the day the last file cabinet was removed from my office. The sensation was even worse the last day I was there. The walls were bare. No more pictures or certificates. I stood in the middle of the room staring out at the patio. Tears rolled down my cheeks. I had been in that office nearly twenty years. Worse, this marked the end of a fifty-year career. To add to the emotions, I felt Nancy next to me. These were heavy moments.

Then it was my turn again.

Earlier in the year my PSA had been checked as part of the normal follow-up procedures. The number had crept upward slightly during the previous six months. Shortly after returning from Europe, my PSA was checked. Again the count had increased. Whereas the urologist aired some concern, the radiological oncologist was more conservative. He felt I should undergo radiation. The two of them conferred on the subject and voted for radiation.

I really didn't need this. I didn't need the worry over the spread of cancer nor the physical effects of radiation. My chief concern focused on why there was any PSA at all. My prostate had been surgically removed and all signs had pointed to clean margins surrounding the gland. Apparently not. The aggressive nature of the cancer and the reason for my having opted for surgery, coupled with the relatively high Gleason score, had indicated a strong possibility that the cancerous tissues had escaped the gland prior to surgery.

The thirty-five week radiation protocol ran well into November. The long treatment period created a problem on the travel front. My daughter and I had clearly drawn from the same gene-pool. We'd no sooner returned from Europe than future travel plans had begun to germinate. My son-in-law just couldn't comprehend our urge. My daughter and I put together a trip to Washington, D.C. and New York over Thanksgiving week. I could only hope that I wouldn't suffer ill effects from the radiation.

Receiving radiation treatments carries a very eerie sensation. Those who've undergone this treatment know there are no physical sensations; it's chiefly in the mind. Even though the X-rays would be focused on a relatively small area, my bladder or part of the intestinal tract could be damaged. The eerie part came from not feeling a thing, yet knowing the rays could be causing damage along with their potential healing capabilities. Would the radiation arrest and kill the remaining cancerous tissues? A new worry had been born.

My last treatment took place just days before our departure. Getting the three of us ready for the trip helped keep my mind off radiation and cancer. Just as during the previous Thanksgiving, I didn't mind being away from home.

My son-in-law was unable to join us so one of my daughters-in-law and granddaughters were added to the entourage. Things went extremely well. The outing was an excellent distraction. Just being away from school, of course, meant the outing was successful for Ed and Scott, and for me as well. As much as I love our home, the challenges and work it represented sometimes surrounded it with a negative aura.

We managed to see quite a bit of D.C. and I think it's fair to say that standing in front of the Capitol building and the White House impressed everyone the most. We were impressed, too, with the very noticeable presence of armed guards around the Capitol; no doubt a result of 9/11.

A visit to the Air and Space Museum was also a high point, particularly for the boys.

New York, of course, had its own charm and flavor. Standing in Times Square at night and taking in a Broadway show were musts. I think, though, the visit to…"ground zero"…the site of the Twin Towers, was the most impressive and, of course, so very sobering as well. It was so difficult to imagine that two huge buildings once occupied this space.

Ellis Island was another site that held great interest for us inasmuch as both my mother and father had passed this way upon arriving in the U.S., my father in 1913, my mother in 1919. Finding my parent's names on the Wall of Honor and locating a prominent display case in which a memento my mother had brought with her from France made the visit that much more inspiring.

This trip was only for a week; still, it was long enough to become annoyed by the not- uncommon bickering between Ed and Scott. This negative side of them seemed to have been increasing in recent months. There had been some of this during the trip to Europe; however, the problem had grown since then. Recalling similar issues among my older children during their teenage years led me to assume that it could be normal. That said, it was still very annoying and I did my best to discourage it.

Just as I had done when returning from the trip to Europe, I started mentally dragging my feet as we headed home from our Thanksgiving trip. On the good-news side for the boys, they had only three weeks of school before Christmas vacation.

That Christmas would be the first we'd stayed home since Nancy's death. During their vacation I made a point of keeping Ed and Scott as busy as possible. This family-oriented time of year could exaggerate the void in our home and lives. Keeping busy was no problem for me. Purchasing gifts and wrapping them kept me busy —no easy task with seven children and seven grandchildren! Nancy had been so good at shopping, wrapping and everything else that went with gift-giving events. She thoroughly enjoyed this side of the Christmas Season.

I have to admit that the gift assignment made me nervous. Maybe I was becoming too old for all of that detail. Also, by nature, I wanted things to be right. No one was to be slighted. There was an understanding among all the parents that the focus would be on the children. Still, trying to match gifts with recipients wasn't easy. Needless to say, my gift wrapping also left a little to be desired.

For Nancy's family, a much smaller clan, gift-giving was much simpler and more practical. The drawing of names meant purchasing only one gift; however, I also had to cover for the boys. And, thankfully, there was a monetary limit. I planned to initiate that concept in the future for my family.

Prior to Christmas I tried to engage the boys in decorating the house. Our hearts just didn't seem to be in it, though. I ended up doing most of the work, the results of which were just okay.

Nancy had possessed a real knack for decorating the house inside and out. She really enjoyed the task and it showed. I didn't even try to touch the outside. Nancy had purchased an incredible number of outside lights. She'd always strung them all over the front of the house.

It was beautiful but I didn't feel up to the chore, at least not that Christmas. Scott gave it a shot and did a reasonably good job.

For the most part, Christmas was enjoyable enough. Following something of a tradition, I had my older children and my grandchildren over for Christmas Eve. It was a noisy and pleasant get-together. The afternoon of Christmas day was spent with Nancy's family. This, too, was enjoyable.

Christmas morning was the toughest time. Four large stockings hung over the fireplace, each with our names on it, including Nancy's. Those of the boys were stuffed with small gift items and the traditional tangerine at the bottom. Nancy would have had a gift or two from Santa on the hearth. Because of the boy's ages – Ed was eighteen and Scott fifteen – I decided they were now too old for gifts directly from Santa.

Opening gifts that Christmas morning was a somewhat sullen and lonely occasion. The previous Christmas in Chicago and Milwaukee had been so lively and memorable chiefly because of the jovial gathering of so many people. I decided I'd somehow team up with one of my older children on Christmas morning the following year.

With the end of the year approaching, it was time for reflection. Once again, what a year it had been: Scott not being allowed to graduate from middle school, all the traveling we'd enjoyed, the sale of my business, and the radiation treatments I underwent due to the sudden increase in my PSA. I'm sure that our having kept so busy during the year helped to significantly diminish many of the vivid recollections of the previous year's tragedy. Also, time was helping to dissolve the effects of our loss.

It was still difficult to read the boys emotional whereabouts, especially Scott. It became increasingly clear that he kept emotional matters to himself. Ed seemed to treat emotional matters in a more matter-of-fact way. On one occasion I commented that I rarely saw him cry. He surprised me by saying that, just because I rarely saw him cry, didn't mean he wasn't hurting inside. He let me know he'd shed many tears while alone. It was a touching revelation. The three of us engaged in much more hugging during the past year or so.

We still had the ongoing problems at school facing both Scott and Ed – and me. In my corner it was the never-ending managing of the household. Any of these could readily lead to anxieties. My stress center, was starting to complain. The aging process and the normal activities of teenage boys exacerbated the problems. I was a tired soul at the end of the day.

Also, during quiet moments, especially at the end of the day, I became increasingly aware of being lonely. At that point it wasn't an overwhelming realization but one that gradually was making its way to the center of my thinking. For so long now my time hadn't been my own; it belonged to others. I wasn't aware of any specific event that might have initiated the realization. Nevertheless, it was there. Late afternoons underscored a very conspicuous hole in my life – not having an adult to share the day's happenings with. Oh, how I missed those wonderful end-of-the-day interludes with Nancy.

Like the previous year, 2004 would prove to be a monumental one as well.

CHAPTER 15

RELIGION, SEX AND OTHER EASY SUBJECTS

2004 opened with a bang! My daughter and son-in-law put on a huge surprise retirement party for me. The number of attendees numbered at least 150. The dye had been cast; I was more or less obligated to give up my professional life.

As Ed or Scott said later, "It was a blast." Yes, it was an incredible evening and I had the feeling that my young sons were impressed with the parade of people who offered kudos for my accomplishments along with the expected mockery and barbs.

In a large sense, the party served as the final nail in my professional coffin. Having sold my files didn't preclude my offering my services as a consultant; I still had my professional brain. However, as time would prove, familial demands absorbed the majority of my time.

I did manage to keep an oar in the water by staying current on the surrounding exploration industry and by jawing with associates.

Ed's graduation from high school in June was a key order of educational business for 2004. Would he make it? It was a challenge all the way. He was struggling, which translated into my meeting with teachers as well as my arranging for a geometry tutor. The boys were not about to allow the education process be an easy one.

A growing amount of the work for school children during the early 2000s involved the computer in one way or another. What a contrast— and a challenge – that was for me. Computers had not been available thirty years for my older children. The same could be said for cellular phones. I'm not sure how young people survived back in the dark ages without either of these technological "necessities".

Another, more troubling comparison between the generations was the advancement of social deterioration, particularly in the raising of teenagers. The 1970s were a continuation of the anti-establishment and permissiveness era. The adage, "If it feels good, go for it," virtually became the mantra of the day. Much of the information about sex and drugs that came out of the closet basically became treated as normal behavior among the younger generation.

Riding herd on my five teenagers had been a monumental task. My more or less conservative ways conflicted with the lure of permissiveness. Attempting to maintain a religious structure within the family was really difficult, all the more so as a single parent. The evolving mood of liberation, which often translated into dissatisfaction within marriages, resulted in more and more divorces. Later, more than one divorce happened within my family and within families close to ours. It's safe to say that this freeing of the soul contributed to my wife of seventeen years having left her husband and children.

Going to church on Sunday became an increasing challenge just as it had been with my older children. I was a life-long Catholic, thanks to my mother having imported the Faith from France when she immigrated to the U.S. in 1919. Throughout my youth, no one discussed whether they would go to church on Sunday. It was a given.

Each of my five older children, according to them, was "forced" to go to church. And what a chore it was getting them to attend. Nevertheless, I managed to have each of them confirmed in the Catholic Church. Today, not a one of them attends Sunday Mass or, for that matter, any form of church-sponsored function. Not only have they given up going to church, two of them purport to be atheists.

Perhaps the apparent demise of the more structured society that preceded the 1960s and 1970s triggered an escape mechanism that affected both the institution of marriage and adherence to religious tenets. Be that as it may, it left a parent, certainly this parent, asking, "What went wrong?"

So many times I gave thanks to my mother for having persisted in not only "forcing" me to go to church but in having introduced me to the essence, the core of the Faith.

Researching the subject as time went on gave me the feel and understanding that positioned me strongly in the Catholic Faith. But it really hasn't helped. So often I feel as though I come across as a real zealot, even though my experience with my older children presumably had taught me to soft-pedal it whenever a discussion entered the religious arena. Where Ed and Scott were concerned, I've asked myself what I could do differently. How could I avoid whatever pitfalls had led to the older children to abandon the church? It seemed as though they had more of a hang-up on attending Mass every Sunday than with the more pertinent tenets of the church. Like the topic of sex, it's not an easy task for the dinosaur I am to discuss the rudiments and requirements of religion with teenage youths. For whatever reason in my case, today's religious challenges haven't changed in thirty years or more. And what challenges they've been!

Along with the computer and cellular era came additional problems. Time and again Ed and I have clashed on the mores of the day, sexual openness and the widespread use of drugs serving as fodder for heated discussions.

Given my age, it goes without saying that Ed thinks I belonged to an archaic era. There was no way he would believe I could comprehend the current social mentality or behavior. It's tough to win discussions – arguments? – on subjects such as young people having sex if they protect themselves, especially if they're "in love." I'm in the very small minority that has no use for young people living together (which I prefer to call shacking up), whether or not they're in love. The idea of marriage seems to be irrelevant.

To Ed's credit, he adamantly refuses to either drink or even try drugs. The fact that he must live with just one kidney led to his distain for any type of drug, medicines notwithstanding. His strong position did not preclude his desire to engage in spirited discussions. It's been as though he has taken on the role of advocate for his teenage counterparts. Either that, or he has just plain enjoyed pushing my buttons for the sake of reaction.

Without question, it was much more difficult to discuss sex and religion with my two boys than it had been with my older children. Society's open and sometimes careless acceptance of sex (including promiscuity), contraceptives, abortion and homosexuality, impose a heavy burden on parents trying to instill moral values in their offspring. On the other hand, however, a mother recently told me she supplied her sixteen-year-old daughter with contraceptives. The rationalization was that the daughter might engage in sexual activities; hence it was better to play it safe and prevent an unwanted pregnancy. So much for abstinence!

During one chat with Ed on the subject of sex, he quickly relegated me to the horse and buggy age. My use of the acronym, VD, brought a puzzled expression to his face. When I explained that it meant, "Venereal Diseases", he climbed all over me. He couldn't believe that I didn't know that these diseases now are called, "Sexually Transmitted Diseases", or STD. I'm afraid I'll be losing many debates.

Another really tough dimension of this early part of the Twenty-first Century is the degrading and debasing music. Rap recordings – these cannot be classified as music – fill young minds with ugly verbiage and content. Add to this the sensual aspects of so many videos and concerts. In fairness, there are many legitimate performers out there and, yes, there are songs that do, indeed, have a melody. But what a chore for a parent!

And what a challenging experience for this seventy-something father to tell his boys about the great music of those "good ole' days." It's an exercise in futility. Ed, who actually does have some appreciation for the big band sounds, and I could go 'round and 'round over present-day "music" and what goes with it. I really get tired of hearing, "Well, it's what young people want; it's what they're buying." And he's right!

My mentioning that they were being brainwashed was futile. I always had fun asking him to hum the melody of a rap number. Given that, basically, there is no such thing, he ended up telling me it's all about the lyrics. Needless to say, that ushered in another round of discussion.

Cell phones and computers offer more notable challenges these days. The time spent in messaging via the various avenues, especially texting, can be incredible. One of the down sides, of course, comes in the form of horrible grammar and spelling habits. Without question, the terrible cases regarding predators and molestations set up through the internet far surpasses poor writing habits.

So many doors to a decadent world have been opened over the decades, that attempting to instill moral values has become a monumental challenge. Adding the attempt to maintain a religious foundation really compounds the problem. Parents in each generation have had to cope with various issues; however, I've found that the mental energy and stamina required to cope with these is far more demanding today for a senior citizen.

Another challenge for me has been learning a new language or, rather, colloquialisms. Because of my two young sons, I've "had to learn" words or terms such as "duh" (response to commenting on a totally obvious point), "rip" (response to a variety of gaffes), "sucks for you" (when something goes wrong for a person), and "don't trip" (apparently derived from "don't trip over your nose"). I've noticed, too, that young people have given up or forgotten the term, "you're welcome". The universally accepted alternatives today include, "no problem", or "no worry".

I'm sure Nancy would have coped much better with the standards of today's generations.

So often my mind has compared today's youth with mine. My younger days covered the 1930s, the Depression years. My father worked at the Douglas Aircraft plant and, ever so thankfully, retained his job throughout the Depression. Still, ours was a frugal life style. We were not in want; however, our existence was basic. Thankfully, my mother was very efficient in managing the household. At ten years of age, following her mother's death, she had been sent to stay for short periods with different relatives in order to learn to cook, to sew and to hand-wash laundry. Above all, she was an extremely skilled seamstress. As much as I admired these skills I was embarrassed to wear the clothing she made for me during my early school years because they weren't cool.

During my youth, endless summer vacations were filled with playing cops and robbers or cowboys and Indians or kick the can or hide and seek. Following the horse-drawn vegetable-fruit wagon or jumping on the ice truck to grab a piece of ice were rituals. It's hard to realize that we'd survived with just an ice box and no freezer.

Roller skating to the next block was venturing into a foreign world. The highlight of the week was going to the movies where we'd be treated to a candy bar, a comic magazine, a cartoon, a chapter in the Lone Ranger series and a full-length movie – all for a dime! And our parents didn't have to worry about our being alone on the streets. And, of course, frequent outings to the nearby Santa Monica beaches were always a treat, sunburns notwithstanding.

Ed and Scott couldn't fathom how we had survived without television Fortunately, there were wonderful radio programs, such leading us to use our imagination: *Flash Gordon*, *The Shadow* or *Terry and the Pirates* in the afternoon; the *Inner Sanctum* or *The Jack Benny Show* or The Ed Sullivan Show in the evenings, and an occasional Joe Louis fight. Needless to say, the breaking news regarding the attack at Pearl Harbor had us all glued to the radio.

It was a simple, uncomplicated time for young people but not necessarily for parents. Yes, my father had a job; however, times were still very trying.

My teen years spanned most of the 1940s – the war years. The early years of that decade were taken up by junior and senior high school. It is interesting to thumb through my senior yearbook and note the dramatic difference in campus attire. Nary a girl is seen in anything other than a dress…a relatively long dress at that. The young ladies weren't allowed to wear slacks or jeans. I've scanned the attire at Ed and Scott's high schools and wonder at the lack of discipline when I see the skimpy garb worn by many girls. Some may call that progress; I just shake my head. The "uniform of the day" for boys was either Levis or white cords and a long-sleeved white dress shirt. And the principal wore a three-piece suit and tie at all times.

Due to World War II, the draft was in effect, with the result that a high- school graduate had the option of enlisting and having a choice of branches and schooling, or of being drafted and accepting what was offered. Upon graduation, I enlisted in the Navy and chose to enter the Combat Air Crewman program. The key and wonderful result of having served, was the golden opportunity to attend college, this followed by my having been able to pursue a challenging career as a Petroleum Geologist. There was absolutely no way that I could have otherwise afforded to attend college had it not been for the G.I. Bill.

Without question, the 1930s and '40s represented an infinitely more moral society. Yes, sex was a forbidden subject, particularly in the home. Drugs? Virtually unheard of. Unfortunately, the word was that "long-haired musicians" were the principal users of drugs. Movies were censored and required no ratings. Manna for parents! Interestingly, the movie censors (the Hayes or Johnson office) forbade husbands and wives to be filmed in the same bed. And toilets were not to be shown in films.

Child molestation virtually was unheard of. The kidnapping of the Charles Lindburg child was a major and unique front-page event. Gangs and shootings at or near schools didn't exist. It was safe for kids to be out after dark. Marriage, to a very high degree, was "'til death do us part." The relatively few divorces seemed to happen mainly in Hollywood.

Clearly, any attempt on my part to draw from the past in a comparative sense was, and remains, largely futile. Each generation will have its good ole' days to refer to; however, in my case, any resemblance between those days and todays truly falls into the apple-and-oranges category. This has been so evident in discussions with my two teenaged, Twenty-first Century boys. It had been easier to span the generation gap with my older children.

Time can erase many negatives from the past. Fortunately, we tend to remember yesterday's good events or experiences. No matter what form of comparison I contemplate, answer typically is, "Give me the good ole days."

As June and graduation approached, nail-biting sessions became increasingly frequent. In order to graduate, Ed had to take an evening class at the same time as his regular classes to make up for an earlier deficiency. But he made it! It was a great occasion. Nancy would have been absolutely delighted. A gathering of family and friends celebrated the accomplishment in proper style.

At this point Ed was nineteen-years-old, a touch older than most high school graduates. This resulted from his having had to repeat kindergarten due to his sessions with chemotherapy and radiation. The logical next step for him was to attend a local junior college in the fall.

Earlier that year my mind shifted to travel — again! The relationship between school schedules and travel had become well engrained because of all the traveling Nancy and I had done. Trying to keep some kind of pace going, the boys and I had used our time-share in Puerto Vallarta during the Easter break. The beach-front resort was beautiful. For the most part, I lounged on a chaise in the shade either near a pool or overlooking the ocean. Working on a tan was not my thing. My younger years included too many horrible burns.

During the week we were there, I read and relaxed more than I ever could at home. I rarely saw the boys during the day, usually because they were around a pool or at the beach trying to impress a teenage lovely. A couple of times during happy hour I sat near a pool-side bar sampling margaritas. Being alone was not pleasurable; I felt out of place. The other adults gathered in pairs or small groups. It was really nice to have a break from my responsibilities, but spending so much time alone started getting to me. Oh, to have had Nancy there.

A month or so after Ed's graduation we teamed up with my daughter and her in-laws for a cruise to Alaska. Again, the break was so good for the three of us, especially for me because I was able to spend a week with adults. Fortunately, the in-laws were great traveling companions.

Nancy and I had cruised these waters years earlier, so much of the trip was a repeat. There was a new stop or two but the combination of relaxing, watching beautiful scenery, and having a lot of fun and laughs made for a memorable outing. Without question, the companionship made so much difference.

Then, over Thanksgiving, the boys and I headed for Disney World in Florida. It seemed as though I was determined to keep the three of us on the road – or was it to keep me away from the rigors of home life?

Basically, the outing was enjoyable. It differed from the trips of the past summer in terms of activities. We were on the move most of the time in the park. The boys, of course, rode many more rides than did

I…and I heard about it! I was labeled, "chicken", more than once. And they were right. I wasn't in need of too many physical challenges.

Sadly, the level of bickering increased a couple of days following our arrival. Accompanying that was the realization that my patience fuse was growing shorter. Also, I began noticing the boy's showing progressively less interest in whatever we were doing. Were their ages a factor? Or mine? Ed was nineteen and Scott sixteen. Even though Ed had a girlfriend, I had the impression that he didn't mind leaving her when it came to traveling.

Invariably, knowing what was on Scott's mind was difficult. His wasn't an expressive or outgoing nature, at least not around me. With my age now at seventy-six, it became increasingly clear that traveling with just the two of them was losing its appeal. Traveling with others, particularly my daughter and her family, was the most enjoyable way. The fact that she handled most of the details related to travel made a huge difference.

Making its way into my thinking also was the question of whether or not I might be overdoing this keep-the-boys-busy thing. I wasn't sure that travel wasn't simply an escape mechanism for me. Part of my think, too, was the likelihood that I had been overcompensating for the loss of their mother. We had passed the two-year mark in March and I was still very keen on keeping her memory alive and on keeping the boys "mothered" and, as well, occupied and as free of concern as possible. Was my way of handling the situation headed in the right direction? Perhaps it was time to re-evaluate. Perhaps it was time for a change.

Included in my thought processes was the feeling that perhaps I was tired of my baby-sitting role. Perhaps, too, going on trips with just the boys accentuated my growing loneliness. The void in my life was expanding and the need for companionship occupied more of my attention. Being aware of this was one thing, doing something about it was an entirely different matter. Was I in the mood to do anything about it?

CHAPTER 16

ED AND THE AIR FORCE

If one thing stood out for Ed during his four years of high school, it was the Air Force Junior R.O.T.C. program. Yes, being a member of the school's band also was important; however, the R.O.T.C.'s discipline, uniform, achievement decorations and the like, became engrained in his psyche. And he was good at it, at least good enough to have achieved the rank of cadet captain.

Two months after graduation, he started attending one of the local junior colleges. As the months progressed it became increasingly clear that the experience was a challenge. It had been his decision to follow this path but disenchantment crept in. Nonetheless, he signed up for the second year to learn more about the elements of the computer world. He had skills in this field.

With growing frequency, conversations turned to the possibility of him entering the Air Force. Discussions were often brief due to the likelihood that he wouldn't be accepted because he had only one kidney. Sure enough, a visit to the local recruiting office confirmed that. The recruiting sergeant turned to the appropriate page in the Air Force "bible" and read that no one with a single kidney would be admitted. No surprise, yet there was obvious disappointment.

Well, we weren't going to just drop the matter. Something had to be done. The challenge was on. I composed a letter to the Air Force Surgeon General pleading Ed's case. We didn't hold our breath.

Surprisingly, the recruiter called several days later to let Ed know that he was being given the opportunity to undergo a physical exam by an Air Force physician. We were impressed. Unfortunately, the results were negative. Even though the answer was logical, it still carried the element of rejection. Well, once again the answer was unacceptable.

There had to be a way. At this point I had to be careful that my mission wasn't personal or ego-related. I stepped back at many points to view the entire forest. Since college didn't appear to be right for Ed, other paths had to be considered. The Air Force occupied first place.

One last effort was in order. In a letter to the U.S. Secretary of Defense I spelled out Ed's medical history as well as his high school experience in the R.O.T.C. and his admiration for the Air Force. I bottom-lined the letter by saying there just had to be a place in the Air Force for the Eds of the country. Certainly, he wouldn't become a pilot; however, in view of his skills with computers, he could be a decided benefit to the service.

Not surprisingly, two or three months went by with nary a word. My letter most likely had found its way either to a wastebasket or was stranded in a pile on someone's desk. Incredibly, a phone call from the recruiter asked Ed and me to meet with him. The first thing he said was, "You must know someone really important upstairs."

Ed was again examined by an Air Force physician. Many nervous moments accompanied the time before, during and after the exam. A few weeks later Ed was notified that, once again, he had failed... however – and this was a huge however – the physician had forwarded the results to the Air Force Surgeon General along with an accompanying notation, "Waiver Recommended". Initially, we weren't sure just what that meant but the recruiter said that, under the circumstances, it was the best news we could have received. I told him, "We'll take it."

A few later weeks later Ed received word that he was to be sworn into the Air Force Reserve, a preparatory step to full active duty.

Excitement was in the air. Because my focus had been so intent on making this work, I really hadn't given much thought to the other side of the coin. His leaving would cast Scott and me into a very different and unknown lifestyle. The more I dwelled on it, the sadder I became.

Without question, I wanted this for Ed. It was such a good fit for him even in the context of making a career of it. Four years was a long time but if it didn't work out, he still had youth on his side. At that point, he was a month short of turning twenty-one. The thought of not being able to celebrate that very important milestone with him was disappointing. Ed told us he'd insist that the basic-training instructors have the Air Force declare his birthday a holiday – which, of course, it was…the Fourth of July.

As the swearing-in date in June approached, the anxiety level started to climb. Yes, I had seen my other children leave home for long periods but this was different. Beyond the new arrangement at home, the thought that Nancy wouldn't be there to witness this most unusual and wonderful event created much sadness.

We had a very fitting going away barbecue. It was happy and emotional at the same time. Adding to the emotions was the presence of Ed's long-time girlfriend. I wasn't sure which would impact him the most; leaving his girlfriend or leaving the comfort of home. I didn't probe and he didn't share his feelings.

During June of 2006, Ed was inducted into the Air Force. Just Scott, my daughter and I attended. His girlfriend was in school. The ceremony took place in a small, paneled-walled, flag-and picture-adorned room. The flags represented each branch of the military while the pictures were of various military figures. A podium stood in the center of a slightly raised platform at the far end of the room. There were no chairs so family members and guests lined the walls.

Prior to the swearing in, the candidates were gathered in an adjoining room. Through a small window in a side door I could see Ed and about ten others sitting at desks as an Air Force officer talked to them. I started to get nervous. The total reality of what I was witnessing, and that which I had helped bring into being, had not completely set in. Was there any way I could get him out of that room?

Within minutes the group filed into the main room and lined up in front of the podium. I tried to keep busy by taking pictures. When the officer instructed the inductees to raise their right hands to take the oath, it became downright emotional. I couldn't hold back the tears. Perhaps I should have been embarrassed but a lot of pent-up thoughts and feelings rushed out. Ed's bout with cancer, the agony of Nancy's passing, and the intensity of trying to live normally after her death heaped together.

I think I stared at his face the entire time. I wanted to pluck him out of the group and hold him and protect him. The manner in which he conducted himself was impressive. He stood so erect and listened carefully to every word the officer said.

My daughter's eyes also were red. Scott's face essentially was without expression. I would have loved to have known what was going through his mind. He would have no one to bicker with now. On the other hand, I felt sorry for him. What would life be like with just the two of us in the house?

Ed's R.O.T.C. experience led to his being placed in charge of his fellow inductees. I could tell he was proud of that, as were we all. The pride and excitement dissipated as the group left for the airport. It was rough. When Scott and I returned home, I immediately went out to our back deck. I knew the scheduled departure time for Ed's flight and, in minutes, the plane appeared not far from our house.

My entire system welled with sadness and loneliness. My watery eyes traced the flight until it disappeared. I cried hard. Scott and I hugged. I couldn't have been prouder of Ed. Nor could I have been more drained. The depth of my feelings surprised me. I wanted him back.

Once again, I had to learn a new mode of living. Obviously, Ed's departure was completely unlike Nancy's when it came to running the household. Several aspects became simpler. Nevertheless, the new emptiness exaggerated the situation. Interacting with just one child was so very different. And, who was I going to argue with? My gosh, Ed wouldn't be there to challenge me on so many subjects. Another cause for sadness.

My relationship with Scott had been different all along. Rarely had we argued. Rarely had he challenged me. His was a much quieter nature. Often, I was curious about why he kept to himself so much. In a sense this new arrangement was good for me. Even though I had fathered seven children, I had virtually no experience living with only one. I had not been particularly good at one-on-one interactions. It had always seemed easier to deal with two or more no matter the situation. This new situation dictated that I quickly learn how to become more involved in my one remaining teenager's life. Changes were in the wind.

Some of the more tangible adjustments came in the kitchen. I learned early that it was easier to cook for three people than for two. Unskilled as I continued to be at the stove, I remained adamant about not succumbing to fast foods. In any event, it would be easier to handle changes in the culinary department than in the loneliness department.

Late that first evening the phone rang – it was Ed. Someone on the bus to Lachlan Air Force Base in Texas had a cell phone. The unexpected call was tremendous. His voice was tired and, if I read it right, slightly apprehensive. I wouldn't hear his voice again for weeks.

The basic training program for the Air Force spanned six weeks. During the pre-enlistment stage, Ed had requested administrative school in Mississippi following basic training. As much as I would have wanted him stationed at one of the bases in Northern California, the thought of visiting him in Mississippi was appealing.

My daughter made plans for us to attend Ed's graduation ceremony at the end of basic training. Well, even the best of plans go astray. The otherwise six-weeks of basic training stretched into eight weeks. Toward the end of the final week, Ed called to announce that he was to be separated from the Air Force. What was he saying? The terminology was new to me. He wouldn't be discharged; instead, he would be separated.

After a couple of phone calls I finally managed to understand what had transpired. At the end of basic training, both parties could evaluate their positions and decide whether there was sufficient compatibility to justify continuing. It was mutually agreed that the two parties would separate. The "marriage" wasn't going to work out. This policy was foreign to me.

The element of surprise wasn't total. Indications were that it was difficult for him to meet the physical demands of the training. I could understand this and I felt so sorry for him. Regardless of the reason, the bottom line was that Ed would be returning home which meant that I would have to return to the drawing board. After having gone to such lengths to break new ground with the military and having agonized over the "giving up" of one of my children, here was another adjustment. But it wasn't about me; it was all about Ed.

I was delighted to have my boy back, yet I wasn't sure how this experience would manifest itself within Ed...or, for that matter, within Scott or me. I certainly didn't want it to be a negative one. I just didn't want him to view this as a rejection or a failure. He'd given it his best shot and it hadn't worked out. The same group that had seen Ed leave, now joined by his girlfriend, greeted him at the airport. We kept the encounter on a genuinely cheerful note. It was so good to have him back.

During the days that followed, I took Ed through my version of a debriefing. Naturally, I was curious about his experience. It was interesting, too, to watch him unpack his duffle bag. Each article of clothing was neatly folded. He seemed proud to show off the skills he'd been taught, like the specific way socks had to be folded to produce a "smiley face." He stayed in basic training mode for days after his return, which was enjoyable.

When asked about the separation, he didn't offer much detail. He voiced complaints about certain members of the training staff and the rigorous physical demands. Otherwise no overriding issue came up as the deciding factor. The experience had impacted him deeply. It was the topic "de jour" for many days. It took a bit of time to ease him back into civilian life.

Perhaps a week or two following his return, a large packet arrived from the Air Force. The letter from the officer in charge of basic training included an interesting passage. It mentioned that Ed could, if he chose, re-apply for enlistment after six months. I assumed that this option was standard Air Force practice, given that it had spent time, money and effort training a person. The effort would not be wasted if that person chose to try again.

So, what was next for Ed? One option received virtually no consideration – school. He wanted a college education but it would have to wait. He realized he had to get a job and start earning money. To my surprise, he came home one day to announce that he'd landed a job in a department store. Although he had to be at work at six a.m., he didn't seem to mind.

It soon became apparent, though, that this type of work left something to be desired. There was no way this would become a career. I was delighted. He was on a learning curve. The experience helped him set his sights higher. For the time being, he was gainfully employed. We would just have to wait and see what tomorrow would bring.

We closed the year with a Caribbean cruise with my daughter and her family. Although not of the magnitude of our trips to Europe, it was still relaxing and fun.

The next order of business was to wonder about the coming year. The big event would be Scott's graduation...we hoped. Would he make it? Could he get it together? Once again, it was nail-biting time.

CHAPTER 17

SCOTT'S TURN

2007 was destined to be another challenging year. The first order of business was for Scott, now eighteen, to graduate from high school in June. Unfortunately, studying was not part of his agenda. Simply put, studying was a drag.

I was seventy-nine and tired. A certain level of energy had leaked from my system. Too much pressure had accompanied my trying to insure that Scott graduated. He had tested both the system and my resolve more than once after his sixteenth birthday. Why he had to stay in high school was an oft-asked question. At his age, he could have dropped out if he'd wanted. He could have taken a job. That attitude wasn't the kind of ambition I needed or wanted to hear.

There was a ray of hope in the area of sports. One of the delights of Scott's junior and senior years was his involvement in soccer and football. I attended virtually every game. It was such a pleasure to watch him on the soccer field. He was such a smart player and a coordinated individual. At the end of the season, he was named to the All-Conference Soccer Team.

His wonderful abilities on the soccer field, notwithstanding, football held slightly more excitement. He was the team's kicker. Because the team often ran up high scores, Scott spent quite a bit of the game on the field, either kicking for points after touchdowns or kicking off. It was a delight to hear the loudspeaker call out his name so often.

As his final season progressed along with his skills, it became clear he could have a future in football. Visions of an illustrious career, first at a top-notch university, then on a professional team played into my fantasies. I pictured myself periodically visiting him at whatever university recruited him.

All of this led to my encouraging him even more to get his act together and graduate. Accompanying this was close contact with his counselor. Mine was a familiar face in the school's office. The game plan – at least theoretically – included Scott taking an evening class as well as a course via the internet. The thought of having to take a summer class coupled with not graduating with his friends seemed to impress him.

Thankfully, once he became seriously engaged in sports, the idea of dropping out, to a point, disappeared; but just to a point. The spring months of his senior year were anxious ones. Somehow, we'd weather the demands of academia while nurturing his athletic skills.

Miracles of miracles, he graduated with his class. My gosh, what we had gone through to get to that point. More than once I had the feeling that I was the one attending school and fighting to graduate? But, alleluia, he would graduate.

As I watched Scott walk onto the football field where the graduation was held, the field that had provided so many exciting moments during the football season, my eyes welled with tears. Nancy should have been there to watch him graduate. Since she wasn't, a degree of sadness was added to the otherwise wonderful occasion. He had a rousing cheering section. For whatever reason, more family members were present than had been at Ed's graduation. Perhaps it was because they were aware of the scholastic struggles Scott had undergone.

Another, slightly sobering thought crossed my mind. Scott was the seventh offspring I had watched graduate from high school. Also, he would be the last. There was a touch of sadness accompanying these thoughts.

As I pondered Scott's future, one thing was clear, because of his so-so grades, a university wasn't in the cards unless, of course, he was sought after because of his athletic skills. Otherwise, he was bound for junior college as was the case with his brother, Ed

Like most graduation ceremonies it was slightly boring and, because of the ninety-degree temperature, it lasted too long. We sweltered in the stands. It was fun to leave the stands and get onto the field once the official, perfunctory announcement was made that the class had, indeed, graduated. While on the field Scott preferred to mingle with his friends, although he did a good job of showing his sincere appreciation to his support group.

Those who had attended came to the house for a brief celebration. Scott had planned to join some of his friends during the evening for their version of celebrating. In the meantime, he had fun opening the many gifts that had been donated to his cause. Cards containing money, needless to say, were his favorites.

Once everyone left and I was alone, I mixed myself a drink and went out onto the deck to relax, sip and reflect. Very naturally, I pictured Nancy sitting next me. I imagined the two of us rummaging around our memory compartments and surfacing at different points on the paths that had led the boys to this point in their lives. I couldn't help but think how very different things would have been had she been with us. Once again the familiar refrain entered my thinking…Why her? Why not me?

While sitting there with my mind in a very definite reflective mode, the value of my circle of friends entered my memory chamber. Whether regarding Nancy's horrible ordeal or the scholastic trials and tribulations of my sons, I often I shared these with my friends at the coffee shop. It was a different form of emotional outlet. I had learned early not to expect too much sympathy from them. Prior to Scott's graduation, these "Monday morning quarter backs" were quick to offer counsel that ranged from "Kick him out" to "Why don't you move out?" (meaning me). The crisp, lightly sarcastic advice helped lighten my load. Also, more than once I told them I was too old to be a housewife. Comments relating to my physical appeal – or lack thereof – were offered rapidly and, of course, with no attempt at finesse. Most important, I drew great comfort from the fact that they "had my back", that they were always there for me. However, any sympathy or empathy offered to me was not going to reach the level of emotional pampering as had Nancy's situation from my friends. They made sure I remained a humble person with their digs and cajoling. I have to assume that the absence of politeness meant that I was one of "da boyz." Without question, those gentlemen possess beautiful hearts.

Yes, another milestone had been reached in our lives; there would no longer be children in mandated schools. We were transitioning from that form of regimented life to who knew what? I tried to envision both boys in a new light, a new context. Certainly, their maturity levels had changed. We were leaving that phase of child-rearing in which the parent was God and in control of their lives. We were entering the phase in which the boys groped for independence. Co-mingled with that was the age-old case of the child progressively knowing more than the parent. That was not easy for this senior citizen to accommodate. They let me know, all too frequently, that my ideas and expectations were from some other planet. Also, it seemed that whatever I had to say, commonly was viewed as a sermon.

Ed's role as the challenger grew across the years. He still loves to take me on regardless of the subject. What a challenge! As often as not, Scott has been there to defend me. I've had the impression he waited for Ed to step out of line so he could jump in and set him straight. Scott loved being significantly taller than Ed. He remembered all those years Ed had called him shorty. More than once I've really felt sorry for Ed. The huge volume of chemicals that were poured into him during his bout with cancer may have affected his height. To his credit, he has handled the matter in a very manly manner.

Scott, on the other hand, has become a much quieter person as he aged. Interestingly, it seems to have coincided with his physical development. When the two of them were in high school, Scott caught up with Ed's height. Four years later he'd reached a height of six-feet four inches, noticeably taller than Ed, a factor that made it much easier to get his brother's attention. Also, it made a difference in his attitude and demeanor. The combination of his nice height and good looks appears to have given him more confidence and self-assurance. Still, he remained a very quiet individual.

During the period prior to and following Nancy's death, the boys were quiet for other reasons; they were frightened and insecure. Then, as now, they spent a great deal of time in their bedrooms interacting with their computers or cell phones. Perhaps the volume of bickering has decreased since then, but unpleasant attitudes frequently arise between them. It was difficult for me to assign this type of antagonism to normal teenage behavior but it was what it was. None of it seemed to be related to the loss of their mother. Then again, I'll never know.

A few weeks after graduation, things got interesting. The football coach from the junior college Ed was attending arranged for Scott to visit the athletic department. Following that visit, I was invited to tour the campus and was given a detailed explanation of the football program. Scott's near-term future was looking up.

The athletic department helped the athletes set up their classes for the ensuing school year. It also provided academic counseling as the need arose. The point that really impressed me was the availability of tutoring should athletes have problems. The coaching staff would make every effort to keep team members from failing.

Although I was impressed, I assumed that the education side of this program most likely would not be of high priority with Scott. Instead, he would most likely tread water, academically, while focusing on football. At that point he indicated no interest in the future beyond junior college.

Disappointed as I might have been, I did acknowledge that many eighteen-year-olds had little clue about the more distant future. Still, I blamed his lack of drive on myself. Why hadn't I been able to instill in him the desire to learn? Why hadn't I done a better job of guiding him? Perhaps it will come to him with time and maturity as it had in my own case.

The fact that Scott was not addressing his future in a manner consistent with my agenda was frustrating. My older children chimed in more than once. Even though each of them had attended a university, they were, for the most part, unified in their counsel that there was nothing wrong with a person not going to college. What would it matter if he should opt to become a mechanic or a bus driver? He would probably go through life with fewer frustrations and headaches.

To me, this clashed with my promise to Nancy to make her proud of him. In retrospect, my insistence that he go to college was pretty naive. Slowly, and with some reluctance, I agreed with my older children. Going to college really had little to do with making his mother proud. With regard to making her proud of our sons, one thing was certain, she would extremely proud of their character, their moral fiber. These were wonderful souls.

During the preceding five years I had been so deeply focused on raising my children and managing a household that the wear and tear increasingly showed. The many details helped to shorten my patience as well as to erode my ability and desire to cope with the myriad demands. While acknowledging these changes, I became aware of a subtle transition.

Age definitely was factoring into my attitude, opinions and outlook – and that translated into a growing level of conservatism. Change was not a friendly word. Whatever the category, I wanted the waters to remain calm. Needless to say, this has led to much frustration. On the one hand, I've had to be as current as possible on young-people thinking (a virtual impossibility!) and topics. On the other, that readily could clash with my old-school "dinosaur" views. How many times have I heard that my opinions harkened from prehistoric times?

Now, with the boys' level of independence expanding, I've become more aware of and sensitive to how I come across to them both in appearance and mentality. As these two gentlemen aged and the future closed in, the writing on the wall grew larger. And it was a scary message; something I just did not want to confront. Another transition was emerging and it was aimed at me. A door to the future was opening progressively wider. I wasn't sure if I were ready for what was on the other side.

An attempt to inch the door open as wide as possible came shortly after Scott graduated. He began airing a subject that did not sit well with me — he wanted to move out. The fact that he'd turned eighteen the previous fall and was an adult, at least in the eyes of the law, apparently excited some new brain cells. He wanted to move into an apartment with a friend. My knee-jerk reaction was, "Forget it." I was still beholden to my parental role.

It was equally clear that he hadn't given a lot of thought to the details of the move; items such as a lease, friends bailing out on a lease, a credit report, and deposits had not been part of his or his friend's planning. Money received but a token comment: Scott's position was that his share would only be $250 a month. And this was while he had no job! College and football would leave him little time to work. He loved being with his friends and moving into an apartment was commonly the priority subject.

Well, nothing was lost by discussing the matter...except that, little by little, one side of the idea began bothering me more. In a sense it was a form of rejection. Did he want to get away from me? A definable hurt accompanied this thought. Was I viewing the move as a bird leaving the nest or as an abandonment of me. Yes, he had pushed the sensitivity button. Self-pity came into play.

During those months, he wanted to be with his covey of friends as much as possible. He stayed out as late as possible and was home less and less. Slowly but surely, that became an issue as well. At eighteen he felt he was free to make his own decisions. This, of course, clashed with my position on ground rules and reasonableness. Attempting to set time limits didn't fly too well. I struggled to remind myself that this drive was normal for a teenager.

Given the fact that during my generation a youngster hadn't become an adult until the age of twenty-one, it was difficult for me to view eighteen-year-olds as adults. Scott was still a child in my eyes. On the other hand, if eighteen-year-olds could enter the military and be placed in harm's way, as well as being able to vote, they were entitled to be treated differently. By the same token, however, he or she should be able to handle responsibilities such as credit cards, cell phones, checking accounts and the like. Well, Scott wasn't quite prepared financially to take on these "necessities" of modern life.

Yes, he wanted to be treated as an adult regardless of how he'd conducted himself in high school and other areas of accountability. But along with this compelling urge to become emancipated arose personal questions. How about me? Where and how did I fit into this equation? Whereas he was seeking independence, I wasn't sure what I was seeking… if, indeed, I was in a seeking mode. His overtures initiated a new thought process for me. Had the time come for me to focus on my future?

Certainly, I wanted a calmer life-style, one in which I wasn't confronted with the endless, virtually daily demands on my energy, time and money. As much as I wanted to sell our home and down-size to a much simpler living arrangement, the depressed real estate market precluded that option, at least for a while. Otherwise, I just haven't had the luxury of planning my own future. Yes, the matter had been touched on along the way. My daughter and son-in-law had mentioned more than once that they wanted me to move closer to them. Without question, the suggestion was gratifying. Down the road it certainly would be an attractive and logical move. For the time being, though, I didn't feel ready to make that sort of decision, at least not until I knew my sons' plans.

Of one thing I was certain: the idea of living alone was a bit frightening. At no point in my life had I lived alone. If I allowed myself to dwell on the subject for any length of time, a mild form of panic set in. I often pondered my mother's solo lifestyle, a period that had spanned close to forty years. For so many of those years she'd been heavily involved in the French colony in Los Angeles as well as in charity work with the Catholic foreign missionaries. With so many activities, it seemed as though she hadn't had time to be lonely.

The bulk of my adult life, aside from professional endeavors, had been dedicated to raising children. I'd remained active in the local oil and gas industry and my primary circle of friends and associates were connected to my profession. However, the industry was a transient one. People came and people went. At their own points of retirement, some chose to settle down in other areas. Troublesome, too, was the fact that my friends and associates were comparable in age. Little by little, the ranks would thin... and that was not a happy prospect.

One common thread in conversations with my older children and friends was living centers that cater to active seniors. This didn't hold an ounce of appeal. It was so difficult for me to think along those lines. With all due respect, those places are for "old people!" How I rationalized the difference between the typical resident in a senior establishment and me at seventy-nine-years of age isn't clear. I have to admit that the older children's push to get me into a retirement community had merit. Their counsel was that I should make decisions regarding my future while I could, rather than have it fall to them should I become incapacitated. They used my mother's situation to emphasize their point.

My mother had lived alone until age ninety-two. Two falls and two fractures of her pelvic bone led my sister and me to take her from her seventy-year residence in Southern California and place her in an assisted living facility near my home. That was extremely difficult for all of us; and certainly, for our mother. She had no say in the matter. Granted, the facility we chose differed from a facility for active seniors;

however, the aura related to that type of advanced-age arrangement chilled me.

Part of my problem, too, stemmed from the intense life I'd known for so many years. Chiefly, my time had been given over to managing the lives of others. Sure, selfishness and self-centeredness on my part cropped up often enough; nevertheless, my mind didn't consider my own future, particularly anything related to my next move or "arrangement." The uncertainties regarding the boys and their futures have protracted any decision-making. On the other hand, have I used them as a shield to avoid making decisions regarding my future? Throughout the demanding times, members of both families offered caring support, especially for Ed and Scott. In particular, my daughter and Nancy's sister gave of themselves endlessly.

With age, I've progressively shied away from the details of organizing get-togethers. Over the years my daughter evolved as the mother hen and social director. Virtually all social events have been orchestrated by her, a task she appeared to thoroughly enjoy. This has freed me of organizational responsibilities for many Thanksgivings, Christmas' and birthdays. Needless to say, my son-in-law's patience and contributions have also been great.

The present had plenty of knowns and predictability. Uncertainties, on the other hand, can really fog up the future. Any way I looked at the situation, too many strings still dangled in front of me to allow me to seriously focus on my tomorrows. Scott was to start college and would turn nineteen in the fall. This would buy me some time. Otherwise, a deep reluctance has accompanied any attempt to anticipate the next chapter in my life. The uncertainties and fears have weighed heavily on me. Other than the knowledge that living alone permanently wasn't too far off, I just didn't want to inquire about what tomorrow might have in store for me. Well, whether or not I wanted to know, I soon would learn what that would be.

CHAPTER 18

ED JOINS TSA
SCOTT MOVES OUT

The relief and high spirits I felt when Scott enrolled at the junior college and started his football career didn't last long. A handful of weeks after school began, it was clear that he would have difficulty becoming the team's starting kicker. A kicker who had transferred from another college possessed experience that Scott had not yet achieved.

Because he wasn't sure if he would realize much playing time, he decided to place himself on the team's "gray squad." The move would preserve his freshman eligibility while allowing him to train with the team. Unfortunately, the plan didn't work too well. He was somewhat deflated, and after a few more weeks we had a long chat during which he mentioned that he wanted to leave school and to get a job. He felt that working for a year would help him get a better feel for his future. Because he wouldn't be able to exercise his football skills, it was clear that the academic side of school would hold little, if any, interest for him. With reluctance, I concurred with his decision. I can't say I was surprised. It did bother me quite a bit that I hadn't instilled in him the spirit of finishing whatever he started. As disappointed as I was, I couldn't force him to go to school. We would just have to take inventory as we went along. Developing a work ethic in the labor force could help both in the experience and maturity departments as well as financially.

Meanwhile, Ed had spent considerable time researching various avenues of employment via the internet. He showed a growing interest in the Transportation Security Agency (TSA), the governmental agency that conducts screening procedures at airports. Perhaps the attraction was an offshoot of all the traveling we'd done. Perhaps, too, his interest was inspired by the uniforms screeners wear. It had been very clear during his R.O.T.C. days that he enjoyed wearing his uniforms.

Ed learned that there was a huge difference between wanting something and achieving it. The application process was highly detailed and demanding. Since TSA is a part of the Department of Homeland Security, it made sense that the screening procedures were rigorous.

An email from TSA congratulated him on his having passed all of the tests. He'd been accepted. Unfortunately, he was being placed on a waiting list. How disappointing. He had no clue how long he would be in a holding pattern awaiting a phone call or letter telling him where and when to report. The situation was vague but that was how the system worked. He considered getting a part-time job; however, that could complicate matters.

Just two weeks later, the phone call came. He was in. He would enter the training program in approximately ten days. What a great relief! What a wonderful phone call. Adding to the good news was the fact that the airport at which he would be trained and assigned was ten minutes from our home. At least some part of his future was looking up.

The positive news didn't stop there. That same day, Scott was hired at a nearby restaurant. Yes, he would start by bussing tables; nevertheless, he would be gainfully employed. Everyone has to start somewhere. He'd already applied at several places with no tangible results.

Upon hearing the news, one of my friends suggested, in jest, that I could start charging the boys for rent. Well…not quite yet.

Perhaps we hadn't entered a new chapter in our lives but we certainly had turned a page. The new page contained some interesting changes, one of which was not welcomed. Once again, it was in the kitchen. In a not-too-gradual way, meal planning, especially for dinner, changed. Scott's job meant he wouldn't have dinner at home four or five nights a week. Ed's interesting work schedule – the 4 a.m. to 12:30 p.m. shift – allowed him to be home for dinner most of the time. Often enough he preferred to dine with his girlfriend, particularly on his days off.

Planning dinner was tricky on those evenings.

As I've grown older, changes in most categories, especially the kitchen, haven't been welcome. Not knowing in advance if I'm to prepare one, two or three dinners can be frustrating, especially if I'm cooking just for me. Unfortunately, I haven't been blessed with innovative or imaginative culinary skills, to which the boys will readily attest. Nevertheless, I try hard to put together healthy meals. The growing disruption with planning meals and from other household chores, no doubt signals a transition to which I'll have to adjust.

One aspect of this new phase is interesting. Perhaps it can be viewed as a preparatory one. Whenever I eat alone and have the evening to myself, I enjoy the quiet time. I am free to do precisely what I feel like doing. However, after a few hours a certain level of loneliness creeps in. Invariably, comfort returns when one of the boys comes home. This could be a stepping stone to the next phase where I'm definitely on my own.

It's anybody's guess how long the transition will last. It's doubtful that both boys will move out simultaneously; at least, I hope they won't. At any rate, I have to keep reminding myself that they are at the starting gate of a phase that will open wide as they ease into the future.

I view Ed's situation in more or less straightforward terms. Now that he is fully employed and possibly embarking on a career, it's likely he'll be the first to move out. Accompanying this is the logical assumption that he and his girlfriend will team up and live together, which will not have my blessing. If he should ask for financial help will I support him? Highly doubtful. If they feel they're mature enough to "play house," they can underwrite themselves. No law mandates that I have to contribute to a cause in which I do not believe. Needless to say, my old-school religious views aren't popular with Ed. How many times has he reminded me that most couples these days live together prior to marriage...if, in fact, they do marry? I guess I'm too old to bend on the subject.

Scott continues to be hard to read and, typically, remains quiet and short on communicating. Now nineteen, he's not a particularly outgoing person, at least not around the house. Logically, he's much more outgoing when he's with his friends. I have asked myself many times if my age, along with the loss of his mother, has contributed to these differences or if it's just a teenage thing. He does possess one particular fine attribute; he shows his respect for me, as well as for all adults, by anticipating helpful needs and in such acts as putting things away. The latter is simple sounding but is so much appreciated.

Ed's personality at nineteen was the opposite. It was difficult to shut him up on too many occasions. He continues to relish verbal duels. He never wants to lose a point. Scott, on the other hand, has often chosen to walk away from negative situations in the house, especially from a dad/Ed debate.

Misgivings continue to crop up when I think about Scott's voiced desire to enter apartment life. I can't get comfortable with the idea. He just seems too young. I'm pretty sure I'd have a different attitude if he shared some definable purpose or target for his future. Whenever the day arrives, I want his move to be a smooth, logical and measured event, one in which I'm able to counsel and assist. An impulsive move likely will cause problems as far as my role is concerned. I'm not inclined to be part of an impetuous venture. Concerns aside, he knows that wherever I call home is his home and that I'll always be there for him.

It might have been Scott's incessant pleas that led me to agree to his moving into an apartment with a friend. Scott was now nineteen, but a very young nineteen. His decision-making capabilities on more than one occasion left a lot to be desired. Perhaps too often, I guess I tended to be pliable, with which I'm sure Ed will quickly agree. As events unfolded, the decision to accept his moving out and into an apartment was the first of several mistakes.

Even before I gave my approval, Scott and his friend had done a reasonably masterful job of mapping out the lay of the land. They had researched several nearby apartment complexes and had their ducks lined up when Scott presented his case. That was all well and good. However, there was one huge hurdle they couldn't negotiate and which they hadn't considered – a credit report. They both had jobs... both at minimum wage...but neither had credit experience.

My daughter and Ed joined me on the day of reckoning at the apartment complex office. A very kind young lady took us through the general paces. Things went smoothly until she reached the bottom line – someone had to co-sign the lease because of the credit report issue. Obviously, I was the logical candidate. Both my daughter and Ed strongly counseled me against signing the lease. Scott and his friend, on the other hand, were laying out gold-plated promises about making good on their end by keeping their jobs and paying their bills in a timely manner.

I signed the lease realizing all the while that I was stretching my neck across the financial chopping block. If the two gentlemen bailed out on the lease and their promises, I would be responsible for the balance of the lease. On the other hand, something inside told me that

I wanted Scott to have this experience. Nothing inside warned me of the experience I was about to have.

Rental payments were due on the third of the month. Well, surprise of surprises, on the eleventh of the third month I received a call from the office letting me know that the boys hadn't paid their rent. The office had contacted them and was told the money was forthcoming. Somehow the money never reached the office. Further, if the money weren't received in two days the matter would be handed over to the apartment's attorneys. My gosh, I couldn't believe that financial problems had started so early.

In contacting Scott, I learned that his friend had lost his job. Scott, had his share of the rent but, unfortunately, the office wouldn't accept partial payment. The signing-day warnings ricocheted around my mind. My role as a co-signer now came into play, a role that soon became a minor nightmare. I paid the bill plus a late penalty and immediately started bracing myself for what I assumed would come next. I wasn't disappointed.

Toward the end of that same month, it became clear that the roommate wasn't capable of handling his financial obligations. Also, Scott asked if he could return home. Sure, I wanted him home, but it wasn't that simple; there was the matter of breaking the lease. As we had been informed on lease-signing day, the penalty for breaking the lease was a month's rent. Very accommodatingly, the office offered to let us amortize the penalty over a multi-month period.

As had been the case at the counseling office at Scott's high school, I soon was on a first-name basis with the staff at the apartment office. One of the staff members clearly remembered my daughter and Ed's admonitions on lease-signing day. Oh well, what could they expect from a dinosaur?

Needless to say, I learned the greater lesson, the lesson having cost me a substantial amount of money. Scott eventually paid me his share; however, his friend was nowhere to be found. When I did encounter him several years later I approached him and let him know that I didn't appreciate his having copped out on the lease. Not expecting to realize a cent from him, I told him that our agreement was to be that, as he made his way through life, he would repay me by helping those in need. He nodded. We shook hands and hugged.

With Scott back home, the ordeal of meal planning confronted me again. A person would think that I would have gained flexibility in the kitchen by constantly dealing with the boy's unpredictable routines. Clearly, the culinary gods weren't about to smile on me.

My "friends" at the coffee shop had quite a bit of fun with this experience. More than once I was asked if I would co-sign some sort of financial matter for them. After all, what are friends for?

Logically, I have to believe that something within tells me that I really don't want to see the boys move out, even though I know it'll come. As rough and tough as our relationships can be on occasion, basically I'm comfortable with the current lifestyle. I've convinced myself that I'm serving a good and valid purpose and am satisfying a necessary role. Certainly, there is ample room for complaints; however, it just seems to be part of the current, comfortable fabric. And, as so often came to mind, I seemed to have carried an on-going obligation to Nancy that I would, indeed, carefully guide our children through the early stages of their lives.

Looking into the figurative mirror, I repeatedly ask myself if my sons are my security blanket. As long as they live with me, I don't have to focus on the future. *Is this what's hidden in my psyche?* On the other hand, I feel it's my duty to put my plans, plans that are foggy at best, on hold until my sons' futures and objectives are better defined.

The relatively difficult life we've known for seven years inevitably will morph into an entirely different one for me. Will it be less complicated; less stressful? Whichever way I look at the situation, I know that my aging body is not looking forward to the expected major change.

Somewhat surprising is that I have precious little recall of my five older children moving out thirty years earlier. Because their departures were spread out over several years and because I met Nancy around the same time, my recall is a bit muddled.

Contemplating the boys' futures brings home how very much I miss Nancy. I just know she would have loved to have been involved in scoping out their futures. I know, too, that the swings in meal preparations wouldn't have bothered her in the least. That happens, in part, when a person has culinary talents.

In a way, Scott's returning home had an element of comfort to it. Perhaps I looked on it as buying some time even though there was no telling how long he would remain. With my mind preoccupied with readjusting to his being in the house, perhaps I didn't have to concern myself with my future – at least not for a while. Once again, was I using my sons to shield me from my future?

CHAPTER 19

THE BOYS' LIVES EVOLVE

As the years have passed by, family matters have taken on different dynamics and directions. The only thing that hasn't changed is that I continue to live in the same house. It was time for sons Ed and Scott to start their futures, their lives taking on interesting dimensions.

First Ed. The urge to move out finally translated into actuality and, not surprisingly, into an apartment with his girlfriend. The move, of course, was without my blessings. Unfortunately for Ed, cohabitating did not last long. The relationship dissolved. Mine was a positive reaction. This was followed by Ed's teaming up with a couple of friends and moving into another apartment which soon became a center for partying. This became a challenge for Ed who still had the early A.M. shift at the airport with TSA.

After several months of this lifestyle, Ed and his roommates decided that he should buy a house, a house large enough to be able to rent out bedrooms. My reaction was, Oh my! Yes, he was employed and, yes, he had received a sizeable inheritance from his grandparents, but was he capable of handling such a significant investment while in his mid-twenties? I let him know right away that I would not co-sign.

But it did happen. Ed bought a five-bedroom house and within a short period had four bedrooms rented out chiefly to friends or friends of friends. Soon, he met another young lady and, after several months of dating, he had her move in with him. All I could do was shake my head. Needless to say, I had no vote in any of this. My days as counsel and guide for Ed were over.

It didn't take long for the housing arrangement to morph into a revolving-door harbor for partiers. Also, it didn't take long for the use of the house to become a giant mess. There was no schedule or rules or regs. The room-rental business was anything but a smooth-running operation.

Then it was Scott's turn. Stilling living at home, he had obtained jobs at two or three fast-food restaurants. In two of them he had advanced to assistant-manager positions which impressed me very much.

The Christmas Eve of 2010 was one to remember. Many members of my family were gathered at my daughter's house. Once it appeared that the exchanging of gift had come to end, Scott walked up to me and handed me a large brown envelope. The envelope received a quizzical look from me. It took several seconds after opening it for the meaning of the contents to register with me. Once I realized what I was holding I about fell over. I was holding Scott's enlistment papers for the Army. It was incredible! I had absolutely no clue that he had done this and that he had done this on his own. It took me and others a fair amount of time to let this sink in.

I was so impressed with him when he explained that he had realized that he really wasn't getting anywhere with his life. Even though he was working and was successful at it, he realized that he was wasting too much of his time and was developing some bad habits. Further, he didn't have a goal for his future. This act on his part was so very impressive and, in short order, took on emotional overtones.

Slowly, I was able to start seeing through the mental mist that had evolved. He had signed up for four years. My gosh, I'll be eighty-six when he gets out; if he decides to leave the service. This life-changing event really rocked my boat. How many times had I said that I couldn't divine the future. Well, here were four-years' worth of it, four years taken care of. Because I had never lived alone in my entire life and with Scott soon to be out of my figurative control, life was about to provide me with a challenge that I knew would someday arrive.

The day came for Scott to be sworn in. My daughter and I were to attend. The emotional recall from Ed's swearing in came rushing forward. I really didn't want to attend; and I almost didn't. For whatever reason I was delayed in getting to the site on time. Scott's voice when he called me asking where I was had a definite gruffness to it. By the time I finally arrived at the building, Scott had already been sworn in. I felt so deeply sorry. But I couldn't leave it as is. I asked at the reception desk if the person who had conducted the swearing in was still available. Within minutes an Army captain approached and introduced herself. She couldn't have been more pleasant or accommodating when she readily agreed to swear Scott in a second time specifically for my benefit. Just the captain, Scott, my daughter and I were present. In my mind and heart Nancy was standing next to me as she had been when Ed was sworn in. This was a very emotional occasion. Once formalities were finished, I don't think I've ever hugged Scott so tightly. Certainly, tears were in my eyes as well as Scott's and my daughter's. To lighten the mood I asked the captain if Scott's having been sworn in twice meant that his enlistment was doubled to eight years. Jokingly, she responded in the affirmative.

More than once that evening, especially in bed, I succumbed to crying. I had a hard time envisioning Scott's new life, a life in which he would have virtually no say; at least during the early phase. Thus far I hadn't given much thought to the new life facing me.

Weeks later, my daughter, Ed, Scott's girlfriend and I attended Scott's graduation from basic training at Fort Campbell, South Carolina. From there we drove him to his next post at Fort Gordon, Georgia, where he would attend a communications school for the following eight weeks.

I was the only one to attend his graduating from this schooling. We'd have to wait to learn of his next assignment.

I don't remember how long it was following graduation that the anticipated phone call arrived. Scott was to be sent to South Korea for a year. I couldn't help but think that my heart had to be pumping hard. He will so very far away. However, and thankfully, he wasn't being sent to Iraq or Afghanistan. In Korea he would be in harm's way, but nothing compared to the Middle East – at least for now. There was even the potential for Ed, my daughter and me taking a trip to visit him and to see South Korea.

During Scott's assignment in Korea, I was introduced to a new piece of technology — Skype. It was great; we could communicate regularly, and face to face. This definitely helped to shorten the distance and loneliness factors.

Also while there, he and his girlfriend developed serious plans to marry as soon as he returned. I played a small "cupid" role in this by arranging for the two of them to meet with the Deacon at the local Cathedral upon Scott's return.

Well, it's hard to imagine that things could have moved any faster than when he got home. He returned on a Tuesday and, with the help of the Deacon, they were married three days later (Friday) and they left for Fort Gordon (Georgia) the following week. It was a whirlwind and blurry set of events.

Within a year, Scott announced that they were expecting. I wasn't surprised and I was pleased. My mind immediately flashed to Nancy and how thrilled she would have been with this news. Knowing her, she probably would have tried to be with the expecting parents for as much as the full term as possible.

When the time neared for the birth, I flew to Georgia just to be there for the two of them. Logically, I wouldn't be much help, but I know that Scott appreciated my presence. Once the two (three?) of them were in the delivery room it was up to me to do the pacing; and I did a lot of it. The delivery took forever with the result that I friended several of members of the staff. From time to time Scott would find me on my well-worn path in the hallway to give me an update.

As it turned out, the delivery was a very difficult one for my daughter-in-law, but a beautiful girl screamed her way into the world. As a result of the difficult delivery, mother and daughter had to spend that and a second night in the hospital. My ninth grandchild (my fourth grand daughter) had arrived.

When it was time for me to return home, I was satisfied that I was leaving this new family in good condition.

Without much fanfare or to do, Ed and his girlfriend married after a year of combined dating and living together. Now it was time to convert their rental house into a home. As time progressed, they gave each tenant notice that the leases would not be renewed.

A few months after I returned from Georgia I was informed that Ed's wife was expecting. It didn't surprise me and, at the same time, I was completely delighted for them. I would soon be running out of fingers when counting the number of grandchildren in this expanding clan.

Prior to the baby's arrival, both Ed and his wife started a business, one that allowed one of them to work from home a high percentage of the time. This would come in handy while raising the baby. And in time, having a parent at home 24/7, offered a very convenient arrangement for raising their beautiful daughter.

Just three months after Ed and spouse started their family, Scott was discharged from the army. Because his wife and now one-and-a-half-year-old daughter had been staying with her parents and, because there wasn't enough room for Scott, he once again came home. It was great having him in our home again even though it would be for a short period only. As things turned out, a month went by before their house-hold goods reached Sacramento. Fortunately, his car had been shipped separately and had arrived ten days after his arrival. Prior to the arrival of their belongings, Scott and his wife had found and leased an apartment, one conveniently located for all family members.

It was time for the three of them to re-unite as a family. However, the size of the family would soon change. Within a short period, they announced that their soon-to-be two-year-old daughter was going to have a brother or sister.

My wife, Nancy, passed away over twelve years ago. Needless to say, she is ever present in our hearts and in our home. Our two boys, both in their twenties, have married and have started their families. I've been in this house for over thirty years and, as one of the boys phrased it, I am now officially living alone. I remain busy with several projects and haven't, as yet, started strategizing my future. I now have twelve grandchildren and two great-grandchildren. I've been remiss by not adequately fulfilling my "Papa" role. Certainly, it will be a significant part of any forthcoming strategy.

CHAPTER 20

REMINISCES AND WHAT'S NEXT?

A new year is in front of us. I just know it will be a pivotal one. In view of all that has transpired during the past many years, I'm reluctant to extend my antennae out too far. Just look at what we've been faced with; all of the negative experiences. But I'm always quick to remind myself that things could have been so much worse. The parade of challenges has served a useful purpose by leaving little time to dwell on the negatives and the hurts of the past.

Then there is the hazy future. Yes, current challenges have to make room for the future. Reluctant or not, it's time to get serious about my own plans. It's not a particularly attractive subject but it's necessary that I give it more consideration. For whatever reason, I've resisted getting a fix on any specific path...not that there are many options.

I'm still glued to the dictates of the parental role. It's difficult for me to shake off the feeling of being needed. The counsel I increasingly received from my older children was to back off and to give Ed and

Scott as much space as they needed. It was a tough piece of advice to follow, but I know it was valid.

My mind tends to treat the matter as a dilemma. Yet anyone with whom I share the issue has the same response — the time has come for me to put myself first. It's time to make decisions that apply to me and my future. This approach is somewhat foreign to me.

I love my home and its river-front setting. But I also know that the time most likely will come to sell the house. I do not know what will follow. For that matter, I'm not sure what type of dwelling I want; an apartment, a smaller house with small lawns? Do I plan for either of the boys or their families needing temporary lodging? Is a retirement facility the best option?

Any future move is likely to be my last, or at least the last in which I'll have a direct say. I'm reminded of a quip one of my friends enjoys repeating: "Be nice to your children; they're the ones who'll decide which care facility you'll end up in." The experience with my mother is a reminder of how readily that can happen.

So very often, especially recently, I've thought about Nancy's outlook for our retirement. She envisioned the two of us moving to a small community in the Sierra Nevada Mountains. She loved the idea of us strolling arm-in-arm each morning to the nearby village to have our morning coffee and to chat with the locals. I have to assume our numerous visits to and around Lake Tahoe were the seed for this bucolic image. For obvious reasons it's difficult to dwell on this, lest it become hurtful. Nevertheless, a very warm feeling accompanies the thought.

Another option, of course, is to remain in the house and to import whatever help, including medical help, I would need, or to have someone offering medical expertise live in the house. At this point, this option doesn't have much appeal for me but, then, I'm blessed to not have serious medical or physical problems at this stage of my life.

Somewhere in my tangled thinking I'm reminded of another time when it was common for married children to have a single parent live with them. That doesn't appear to be an option in my case. Anyway, it's not a scenario that's appealing at this time. My dislike of living alone adds to the dilemma. The idea mentioned before, being close to one of my children, has merit. Any way I look at it, dwelling on future lodging only leads to frustration.

Meanwhile, I hope and pray I won't be a burden on my children down the road.

Now that I'm ninety, the horizon can be gloomy if I dwell on this aspect of the future. Fortunately, I don't feel the age represented by the number that dates me. I've been blessed with an above-average level of energy, an outgoing personality, and a pretty good sense of humor. And I am so very fortunate to be in the physical shape I'm in. My mind remains sharp (most of the time!) even though the memory factor needs readjusting from time to time, and I cope very well with my daily needs and responsibilities. Occasionally, however, my curious mind will probe the longevity question regarding much time do I have left. Obviously, I don't dwell on this. It will be what it will be. It's always nice to have someone show surprise when they learn how old I am. Jokingly, I tell them I'm going to include them in my will. I keep reminding myself that I have so much to be thankful for.

It will be interesting to experience days with few or no obligations. For so many years now, the majority of my time has not been my own. It's been so easy to ask, "Free time? What's that?" I'll have plenty of it down the road. Fortunately, there will be no shortage of projects; I'll have plenty to do. The bottom line is, I'll just have to wait to see which direction the fickle finger of fate will point.

One of the key aspects of the unusual arrangement of my life is the sadness that hits me when I realize that the boys could be parentless at a relatively early age. I don't envy them. They've done nothing to deserve that. But they do deserve to have their mother sharing in their lives. I've felt all along that they would have been so much better off if the reverse had been the case. This really saddens me. Needless to say, I'll keep myself in the best shape possible both for their sake as well as my own.

Also, I have felt a real emptiness when I think about Nancy not having been here when her sons married and fathered children. She would have loved to have helped with wedding preparations and, above all, to be there for the birth of her grandchildren. She so loved children. Yes, thinking about all of this can bring forth sadness and, frequently, tears.

As for relocating near one of my children, young or old, the thought of becoming better acquainted with my many grandchildren crosses my mind. Having fathered children at an advanced age has led to a strange situation. At the time Ed and Scott were entering the world, my older children were also giving birth to and rearing children – my grandchildren. Accordingly, my mind never really settled on the fact that I, indeed, am a grandfather. It just hasn't wanted to fit.

Often, I've sat in the coffee shop and listened to my friends comment on and brag about their grandchildren. It's somewhat foreign to me. We've had some laughs when I've mentioned the confusion that arises when my youngsters try to figure out which kids are cousins or who is an uncle to whom. Perhaps I'll take on the grandfather role now that Ed and Scott have children, as ill prepared as I am.

I really never knew my grandparents. My father and mother immigrated to the United States at relatively young ages – each of them at or near 20. I visited my maternal grandfather, who was a native of France, when I was two-years-old; hence I have no recollection of him except from pictures. My maternal grandmother passed away when my mother was but ten-years-old. My paternal grandfather, a native of the Isle of Man (United Kingdom) passed away even before my father came to America. I had the pleasure of meeting my charming paternal grandmother on a visit to the Isle. She was in her nineties, I was in my early twenties. Clearly, I will have much to learn in the grandfathering department.

I try to visit Nancy's (and my mother's) gravesites regularly with fresh flowers. Both ladies loved flowers. One of Nancy's pleasures and source of pride was her beautifully kept garden. Visiting family gravesites is a tradition my mother brought with her from France, a tradition she instilled in my sister and me at an early age. While at the cemetery, I often ponder Nancy and my lives together and the incredible experiences we had along the way. It's so easy for the experiences to be recycled over and over again. How impressed I was that Nancy showed virtually no hesitation in marrying an older man. Our riverfront life coupled with professional passions and travel provided us with an enviable lifestyle.

Then again, how can a person know what awaits them? There was absolutely no way we could have anticipated Ed's lengthy struggle with cancer. It was a horrible yet humbling experience. But when the result is a cancer survivor, the word, *blessed,* takes on a deep significance.

To watch a mother and wife slowly die over a nine-month period, from the summer of 2001 to early 2002 can only be described as tragic. And what can be said about a widowed father in his seventies trying to parent two young boys through their demanding school and teenage years? All of these situations lead to that oft-repeated question: "Why her? Why not me?"

Frequently I ponder whether I would recommend an older man marrying a younger woman. Even though marriages between partners of disparate ages are not uncommon, the question is a fair one. It would, to a point, depend on the difference in ages and the age levels. I would probably advise against it if the couple intended to have children, again depending on the man's age. Important elements that factor in when considering the advisability of an older man fathering children, include health, financial security and availability of family support. Without question, the older male also must be endowed with a deep reservoir of patience, all the more so if he should become a single parent.

Also, can a significantly older father negatively affect his children, particularly in their younger years? No one wants to be an embarrassment to their offspring. Whether my age and or my appearance has been or is a problem for Ed or Scott, I've seen no indication of this. My mind and heart tell me it really hasn't been an issue, but who knows what goes on in their mind and heart?

In my case, age was rarely discussed. Very importantly, neither the age difference between their mother and me nor the awareness that I was much older than other fathers never seemed to be a concern. Part of this may have stemmed from the fact that I was who I was from the first day of their lives.

If I had to do it over again, would I marry a younger woman? Without question…if I were so blessed to meet another Nancy. Not surprisingly, love and respect override many practical factors. Most likely, I would treat the matter on a case-by-case basis. The logical follow-up question is whether or not I would be in favor of fathering children in my late fifties? A difficult question. Even in the context of all the trials and tribulations I experienced as a single parent, I can't envision life without Ed and Scott, both of whom I love so dearly. But would I recommend a fifty- or sixty-something man fathering children late in his fifties? I think not. Too many variables and unknowns exist. How can a person predict the future? In my case, the previous experience of having been a single parent and having struggled in raising five children, different as it had been, had its rewards. Each of them became very successful. Even then, the rigors of raising young sons at my advanced age have been incredibly demanding. The differences between generations from the standpoint of mores, fads and, in particular, morality can be huge and, in my case, often was very difficult to handle.

Today's society is vastly different from the one in which I grew up or even the society in which my older children were raised. For example, it is so difficult for a person of my generation to understand the level of killings within families, at schools and on our streets today. A murder was front-page news from the 1930s into the 1950s. Today, virtually each page of a newspaper carries one or more articles related to murders or violence. Further, the steady deterioration in the morality in this country also is cause for great concern.

Discussing sex with my children, in particular, has been a tricky subject because it was a taboo subject at all levels in my youth. Neither my father nor my mother sat me down for a birds-and-bees discussion. Similarly, I doubt that I engaged in discussions regarding sex with my older children. It's been difficult for me across the years to ease into the mainstream of current thinking and expression.

Furthermore, a high degree of my views are rooted in the Catholic Faith with the result, perforce, that my assessments continue to be on the conservative side. Logically, my position isn't too popular with my sons.

We've "progressed" from the sterile movies of the 1930s and 1940s to films in which sex is a principle thread for most story lines. And then there's violence, be it in films, television or arcade games. It's so difficult to guide young people through the mine fields that society has placed in front of them today. I do not envy our youth.

Drugs and alcohol, of course are interesting subjects. As mentioned earlier, Ed, who is so protective of his single kidney, has no use for any form of drugs or alcoholic beverage. Scott, on the other hand, will speak positively about the benefits of marijuana. Of course, the widespread availability of marijuana for "recreational use" has shed an entirely different light on it. Thankfully, it has great potential in the world of medicine. As for alcohol, Scott doesn't see any harm in an occasional beer…or two. Actually, I enjoy having one with him.

Tattoos and body piercings form another center piece for discussions, especially with Scott. Against my wishes, but in the context that he was over eighteen, he had his ears pierced. Fortunately, the earrings he wore were tasteful enough. Somewhere in there, and unbeknownst to me, he squeezed in a tattoo. He had a heart dedicated to his mother tattooed on his chest above his heart. What could I say? It was a loving act. I do have to ask the question: what in the world is it with these young people? I will never understand the urge to deface their body. Obviously, they are unaware of the shriveling skin that awaits them later in life.

I can't remember a single male having tattoos or wearing earrings in any of the schools I attended. Similarly, and fairly surprising, I don't recall too many men with tattoos while I served in the World War II navy. Even then, the tattoos commonly were small and usually hidden under clothing. Many of today's massive tattoo designs are works of art.

I do know that challenges to my decisions or viewpoints can affect me. Being challenged certainly can bruise the ego. That's nothing new. I can remember being party to many verbal scuffles with my older children during their late-teen years. It has to come under the heading of another teenage thing. Ed frequently will come up with a smart-mouthed quip regarding my horse and-buggy or dinosaur ideas. It's okay as long as he keeps it on the light side. Often enough I have to remind him about the commandment, *honor your parents*. I wear hearing aids and, from time to time, I hear, "Come on, dad, crank up your hearing aids." I have to admit that, occasionally, I do miss out on what's being said. But I don't need this guy letting me know about it!

It also bothers me that the two of them can be mean to each other so much of the time. It makes a person wonder if, indeed, they are brothers; or maybe that's why.

An important aspect of the aging process that factors in here is my becoming increasingly set in my ways. I know this has a universality to it. So much of my daily life can be patterned or habitual. Detouring from my routines can be frustrating. I've tried hard to work around much of that in deference to my sons.

As we ease into the new year, I continue to ponder the changes that I've had to face, such as losing control over my son's lives. I believe that any control I had was borne from my high-order protective nature. The two of them had labelled me as a certified world-class worry wart.

The frustration of not knowing how to handle meal continues; however, this concern is secondary to a growing loneliness. I do enjoy having time to accomplish certain projects without interruption. But when the sun goes down, evenings can exaggerate loneliness. It's always a treat when I'm invited for dinner by one of my children or a friend.

Even finding myself at the leading edge of a major change in my life, I frequently ask myself if I did enough to prepare Ed and Scott for their futures. Some inner voice says that I haven't. Because it had been so challenging to maintain our home and to have overseen their daily lives, many essentials have been bypassed. I can't help but believe that much of this was due to my having felt so sorry for them and to my dedication to make life as normal and pleasant as possible. Also, another probable disservice consisted of my finding it more expeditious for me to get something or to do something on my own rather than to argue over which of the two should help. That has not served them well. Hopefully, they have found a counterpart who possesses those skills.

The protective shield I've had around them all these years is no longer necessary. One aspect of my "housewife" days does linger; I know I'll miss caring for them when they're sick. Whenever they've been sick, something inside of me automatically clicks. Caring for them has been paramount; nothing else mattered. Perhaps it's a case of my feeling needed and useful.

Along with all of its sadness and unpredictability, life has been incredibly good to us. We have all been so blessed, including Ed's terrible battle with cancer. I kept logs of each of our travels and decided a few years back to compile an itemized list of all trips to foreign lands. It didn't matter who was on the trips. I was so impressed that the list showed that we had been to Europe 24 times and had visited 38 countries around the world. Indeed, we have been so incredibly blessed. Mention must also be made that our lives have been gifted with an abundance of love.

My memories of Nancy still remain vivid. I've wondered more than once if something else could have been done for her. Should we have sought a second opinion at a world-class cancer center? I've had to assure myself that the treatments and protocols she received were the best available. I do know that her principal oncologist was a class act. I will always be amazed at just how fast the murderous cancer raced through Nancy's body.

The current chapter in the boys' and my lifes basically has closed. The three of us have done a lot together and we've had our ups and downs as well as a lot of fun. Perhaps these two guys helped me feel younger. A new chapter is opening inasmuch as change very definitely is in the air and a certain amount of obvious, figurative writing is growing larger on the wall. I'm not looking forward to the expected significant changes that, realistically, will have to occur but, at the same time, there's little I can do to alter inevitability. Without question, I'm curious to learn how I'll handle the lifestyle that lies ahead, unknown as it is, as well as the release of the pressure of responsibilities I've had for so many years.

I will continue my many projects and my teaming up with my retired oil-industry friends and, of course, I will dedicate myself to my role as a grandfather and great-grandfather. And, for some convoluted reason, I might even look forward to occasionally locking horns with my son, Ed. There is a very clear and greatly appreciated side of Ed that makes up for much of the rough stuff he throws at me – he has my back. Engaging in hot discussions with him might be viewed as a form of mental exercise; however, I'm not sure how good it is for my heart.

The rest I will leave to my Creator.

About the Author

Roland Bain was a "Great Depression baby", having been born in Los Angles, California in 1928. After graduating from Los Angeles High School, he enlisted in the Navy near the end of World War II. Following his discharge, he attended UCLA where he earned his Master's Degree in petroleum geology. While at UCLA he joined the Beta Theta Pi fraternity, becoming its president in his senior year. In 1956, Roland was awarded a Fulbright Scholarship to study at the Sorbonne and to conduct research at the French Petroleum Institute near Paris, France.

His first employment was with Texaco Corp. where he became engaged in the search for oil and gas accumulations in the Los Angeles Basin. Two years later he was transferred to Sacramento where he spent the following seven years conducting similar research. Leaving Texaco, he became a Consulting Petroleum Geologist and was successful in developing several impressive accumulations of natural gas. His expertise resulted in his consulting for such entities as the Pacific Gas &Electric Co., Dow Chemical and the Sacramento Municipal Utility District.

Roland's publishing credits include two published books - HOLLYWOOD DECO FASHIONS OF THE 1920s, a heavily illustrated fashion-design book about his mother's arrival from France in 1919 and her becoming a costume designer in Hollywood's movie industry during its1920's Golden Age, and _ENTER THE ENEMY, A French Family's Life Under German Occupation_. Other publishing credits include a seven-year stint as a columnist for The Sacramento Union (the oldest daily newspaper west of the Mississippi), and numerous published professional articles. His dedication to professional reporting earned him honorary life-time memberships in two professional associations.

Printed in the United States
By Bookmasters